FAIR PRACTICES
IN HIGHER EDUCATION

*Rights and Responsibilities of Students
and Their Colleges in a Period of
Intensified Competition for Enrollments*

*A report of the
Carnegie Council
on Policy Studies
in Higher Education*

FAIR PRACTICES IN HIGHER EDUCATION

*Rights and Responsibilities of Students
and Their Colleges in a Period of
Intensified Competition for Enrollments*

Jossey-Bass Publishers

San Francisco • Washington • London • 1979

FAIR PRACTICES IN HIGHER EDUCATION
*Rights and Responsibilities of Students and Their Colleges
in a Period of Intensified Competition for Enrollments*
The Carnegie Council on Policy Studies in Higher Education

Copyright © 1979 by: The Carnegie Foundation
for the Advancement of Teaching

Jossey-Bass Inc., Publishers
433 California Street
San Francisco, California 94104

Jossey-Bass Limited
28 Banner Street
London EC1Y 8QE

*This report is issued by the Carnegie Council on Policy Studies
in Higher Education with headquarters at 2150 Shattuck Avenue
Berkeley, California 94704.*

*Copies are available from Jossey-Bass, San Francisco,
for the United States and Possessions, and for Canada,
Australia, New Zealand, and Japan.
Copies for the rest of the world available from
Jossey-Bass, London.*

Library of Congress Catalogue Card Number LC 79-84232

International Standard Book Number ISBN 0-87589-415-1

Manufactured in the United States of America

JACKET DESIGN BY WILLI BAUM

FIRST EDITION

Code 7915

The Carnegie Council Series

The Federal Role in Postsecondary
Education: Unfinished Business,
1975-1980
*The Carnegie Council on Policy
Studies in Higher Education*

More Than Survival: Prospects for
Higher Education in a Period
of Uncertainty
*The Carnegie Foundation for the
Advancement of Teaching*

Making Affirmative Action Work
in Higher Education: An Analysis
of Institutional and Federal
Policies with Recommendations
*The Carnegie Council on Policy
Studies in Higher Education*

Presidents Confront Reality: From
Edifice Complex to University
Without Walls
*Lyman A. Glenny, John R. Shea,
Janet H. Ruyle, Kathryn H. Freschi*

Progress and Problems in Medical
and Dental Education: Federal
Support Versus Federal Control
*The Carnegie Council on Policy
Studies in Higher Education*

Faculty Bargaining in Public
Higher Education: A Report and
Two Essays
*The Carnegie Council on Policy
Studies in Higher Education,
Joseph W. Garbarino, David E.
Feller, Matthew W. Finkin*

Low or No Tuition: The Feasibility
of a National Policy for the
First Two Years of College
*The Carnegie Council on Policy
Studies in Higher Education*

Managing Multicampus Systems:
Effective Administration in an
Unsteady State
Eugene C. Lee, Frank M. Bowen

Challenges Past, Challenges
Present: An Analysis of
American Higher Education
Since 1930
David D. Henry

The States and Higher Education:
A Proud Past and a Vital Future
*The Carnegie Foundation for the
Advancement of Teaching*

Educational Leaves for Employees:
European Experience
for American Consideration
*Konrad von Moltke,
Norbert Schneevoigt*

Selective Admissions in Higher
Education: Comment and
Recommendations and Two Reports
*The Carnegie Council on Policy
Studies in Higher Education,
Winton H. Manning, Warren W.
Willingham, Hunter M. Breland,
and Associates*

Investment in Learning: The
Individual and Social Value of
American Higher Education
Howard R. Bowen
with the collaboration of Peter
Clecak, Jacqueline Powers Doud,
Gordon K. Douglass

Missions of the College Curriculum:
A Contemporary Review with Sug-
gestions
The Carnegie Foundation for the
Advancement of Teaching

Handbook on Undergraduate
Curriculum
Arthur Levine

Curriculum: A History of
the American Undergraduate
Course of Study Since 1636
Frederick Rudolph

The States and Private
Higher Education: Problems
and Policies in a New Era
The Carnegie Council on Policy
Studies in Higher Education

Fair Practices in Higher Education:
Rights and Responsibilities of
Students and Their Colleges in a
Period of Intensified Competition
for Enrollments
The Carnegie Council on Policy
Studies in Higher Education

The following technical reports are available from the Carnegie
Council on Policy Studies in Higher Education, 2150 Shattuck Avenue,
Berkeley, California 94704.

The States and Higher Education:
A Proud Past and a Vital Future
SUPPLEMENT to a Commentary of
The Carnegie Foundation for the
Advancement of Teaching
The Carnegie Foundation for the
Advancement of Teaching

Federal Reorganization:
Education and Scholarship
The Carnegie Council on Policy
Studies in Higher Education

A Classification of Institutions
of Higher Education: Revised
Edition
The Carnegie Council on Policy
Studies in Higher Education

Carnegie Council National
Surveys 1975-76: Undergraduate
Marginals (Vol. 3)
The Carnegie Council on Policy
Studies in Higher Education

Changing Practices in
Undergraduate Education
Robert Blackburn, Ellen
Armstrong, Clifton Conrad,
James Didham, Thomas McKune

A Degree for College Teachers:
The Doctor of Arts
Paul L. Dressel, Mary Magdala
Thompson

Carnegie Council National
Surveys 1975-76: Faculty
Marginals (Vol. 2)
The Carnegie Council on Policy
Studies in Higher Education

Carnegie Council National
Surveys 1975-76: Graduate
Student Marginals (Vol. 4)
The Carnegie Council on Policy
Studies in Higher Education

Enrollment and Cost Effect of
Financial Aid Plans for Higher
Education
Joseph Hurd

Market Conditions and Tenure for
Ph.D's in U.S. Higher Education:
Results from the 1975 Carnegie
Faculty Survey and Comparison
with Results from the 1973 ACE
Survey
*The Carnegie Council on Policy
Studies in Higher Education*

Field Disaggregated Analysis
and Projections of Graduate
Enrollment   and Higher Degree
Production
Christoph von Rothkirch

Market Conditions and Tenure in
U.S. Higher Education 1955-1973
Charlotte V. Kuh

U.S. Faculty After the Boom:
Demographic Projections to 2000
Luis Fernandez

Preserving the Lost Generation:
Policies to Assure a Steady Flow
of Young Scholars Until the Year
2000
Roy Radner, Charlotte V. Kuh

Contents

Preface

The ethical conduct of higher education has been a continuing concern of the Carnegie Council. Our interest in this essential aspect of the academic community has been particularly expressed in several reports: Most recently, in *Missions of the College Curriculum* (1977), we discussed the "moral values" that should animate instruction. In two reports, *Selective Admissions in Higher Education* (1977) and *Making Affirmative Action Work in Higher Education* (1975), we treated the ethical components in policies for equality of opportunity. The latter concern carried on a tradition of the predecessor Carnegie Commission which issued reports on *A Chance to Learn* (1970), and *Opportunities for Women in Higher Education* (1973).

Both the Council and the Commission have at all times sought to advance the cause of educational justice for the postsecondary age group. Other reports of the Commission in the area of ethical conduct have been: *Dissent and Disruption* (1971) which, among other things, set forth a model "Bill of Rights and Responsibilities for Members of the Campus"; *Reform on Campus* (1972) which suggested that greater attention be paid to the principles embodied in what was called the "unwritten academic constitution"; and *The Purposes and the Performance of Higher Education in the United States* (1973) which sought to set up some guidelines for the proper conduct of the important purpose of "evaluation of society for self-renewal."

Thus, this report on "Fair Practices" seeks to extend earlier comment upon and advice about the proper ethical condition of higher education.

Council discussions benefited from comments on early drafts of this report given by George Arnstein, consultant to the Veterans Administration; Elaine El-Khawas, director, Office of Higher Education Self-Regulation Initiatives, American Council on Education; Steve Jung, senior research scientist, American Institutes for Research; Richard Millard, director, Division of Postsecondary Education, Education Commission of the States; Theodore Marchese, director, Institutional Research, Barat College; Layton Olson, vice-president, National Student Educational Fund; John Proffitt, director, Division of Eligibility and Agency Evaluation, U.S. Office of Education; David Riesman, Henry Ford II Professor of Social Sciences, Harvard University; and Kenneth Young, president, Council on Postsecondary Accreditation. None of these advisers, of course, is in any way responsible for the findings or conclusions of this report.

We wish to express appreciation to Arthur Levine and Keith Wilson for their assistance in preparation of the report.

Members of the Carnegie Council on Policy Studies in Higher Education

Nolen M. Ellison
President
Cuyahoga Community College

Nell Eurich
Senior Consultant
International Council for Educational Development

Daniel J. Evans
President
Evergreen State College

E. K. Fretwell, Jr.
Chancellor
The University of North Carolina at Charlotte

Margaret L. A. MacVicar
Associate Professor of Physics
Massachusetts Institute of Technology

Frank Newman
President
University of Rhode Island

Robert M. O'Neil
Vice-President
Indiana University at Bloomington

Rosemary Park
Professor of Education Emeritus
University of California, Los Angeles

James A. Perkins
Chairman of the Board
International Council for Educational Development

Alan Pifer
President
The Carnegie Foundation for the Advancement of Teaching

Joseph B. Platt
President
Claremont University Center

Lois D. Rice
Vice-President
College Entrance Examination Board

William M. Roth
Trustee
Carnegie Institution of Washington, D.C.

Stephen H. Spurr
Professor
LBJ School of Public Affairs
University of Texas

Clark Kerr
Chairperson
Carnegie Council on Policy Studies in Higher Education

FAIR PRACTICES
IN HIGHER EDUCATION

*Rights and Responsibilities of Students
and Their Colleges in a Period of
Intensified Competition for Enrollments*

1

General Comments

Fair practice has been a basic and continuing theme of American higher education since the founding of Harvard in 1636. Colleges and universities have taught and practiced moral and civic virtues throughout our national history, have sought to advance the truth, and have been devoted to public service. Their members often have served as the conscience of the nation. The academic virtues are a model for the conduct of society at large. They include respect for facts and careful analysis; civility in argument; careful consideration of alternative points of view and of solutions to problems; and reliance on persuasion.

Positive Aspects of Student and Institutional Conduct

In recent times, higher education in the United States has made many contributions to ethical conduct:

- By greatly expanding equality of opportunity in higher education
- By maintaining the academic "value added" for its students even as it seems to have gone down substantially for many graduates of our high schools
- By serving as a forum for discussions of many national issues such as civil rights, the war in Vietnam, and the physical environment
- By serving students in a manner that leaves most of them satisfied with the college they are attending, thereby providing a valuable model for other social institutions

Evidence of these and other "positive aspects" of ethical conduct in higher education discussed in this report may be summarized as follows:

1. *Students are very serious about their schooling.* Eighty-one percent of undergraduates say they work hard at their studies and 79 percent believe hard work always pays off (Carnegie Surveys, 1975-76).[1]

2. *Students are satisfied with the instruction they receive.* Seventy-two percent of undergraduates report that they are satisfied with the teaching they have had at college (Carnegie Surveys, 1975-76).

3. *Faculty are generally available to students.* Ninety-one percent of college and university faculty have scheduled office hours and 64 percent of undergraduates say there are professors who take a special interest in their academic progress (Carnegie Surveys, 1975-76).

4. *Students trust their teachers.* Seventy-six percent of undergraduates say that on the whole they trust the faculty at their college to look out for students' interests (Carnegie Surveys, 1975-76).

5. *Students are satisfied with the academic programs they have taken.* For example, 77 percent of undergraduates report satisfaction with their major programs and 57 percent are satisfied with the grading system and evaluation at their colleges (Carnegie Surveys, 1975-76).

6. *Both faculty and students are committed to developing ethical values in college.* Eighty-two percent of college and university faculty believe that firm moral values are an important consequence of education and 93 percent of undergraduates think it is essential or fairly important to formulate values during college (Carnegie Surveys, 1975-76).

7. *Students are satisfied with the college they are attending.* Seventy-one percent of undergraduates report they are satisfied or very satisfied overall with their school (Carnegie Surveys, 1975-76).

---

[1]The Carnegie Council studies cited throughout this report are described in Appendix B.

8. *Students are learning as much as ever.* Despite continuing declines in the qualitative and quantitative scholastic aptitude test scores of high school seniors, the "value added" by college has remained constant or increased over the years since 1966 as measured by scores on the graduate, business, and law school admission tests (Manning, 1976; Boldt, 1977).

9. *Colleges are improving the state of educational justice.* Achievements include an increase in college attendance rates for blacks (from 4.6 percent in 1967 to 10.7 percent in 1976), women (from 34.9 percent in 1967 to 43.2 percent in 1976) and the poor with family incomes under $5,000 per year (from 20 percent in 1967 to 22.4 percent in 1976) (U.S. National Center for Education Statistics, 1978). Moreover, 69 percent of American institutions of higher education have special recruiting programs to attract adults over 22, part-time students, minorities, or disadvantaged students (Carnegie Surveys, 1978).

Negative Aspects of the Conduct of Higher Education

Yet we are concerned. We see certain signs of deterioration of important parts of academic life, and in particular:

- A significant and apparently increasing amount of cheating by students in academic assignments
- A substantial misuse by students of public financial aid
- Theft and destruction by students of valuable property, most specifically library books and journals
- Inflation of grades by faculty members
- Competitive awarding of academic credits by some departments and by some institutions for insufficient and inadequate academic work
- Inflated and misleading advertising by some institutions in the search for students

Most institutions of higher education, to a small or large degree, exhibit one or more of these destructive aspects. Evidence of these and other "negative aspects," which is discussed in more detail later in this report, includes the following:

1. *Financial aid abuse.* Thirteen percent of the loans made
   under the Guaranteed Student Loan program are in default
   ("HEW to Step Up Collection of Direct Loans," 1978).
   Seventeen percent of the National Direct Student Loan recipients are also in default ("Two-Year Colleges Lead in
   NDSL Defaults," 1978). The rate of nonrepayment of the
   intentionally high risk veteran's loans is 44 percent. And
   1,600 Guaranteed Student Loan borrowers and 20,245 National Direct Student Loan recipients have filed for bankruptcy to discharge their loans ("Senate Panel Clears Ban on
   Student Loan Bankruptcies," 1978).
2. *Academic dishonesty.* This ranges from cheating to theft and
   destruction of library materials. With regard to cheating, 8.8
   percent of undergraduates report that some forms of cheating are necessary to get the grades they want. That is an increase of 1.3 percentage points since 1969. At research universities, the proportion of students responding in this
   manner rose from 5.4 percent in 1969 to 9.8 percent in
   1976 (Carnegie Surveys, 1969-70; 1975-76). And larger percentages of students admit to more spontaneous forms of
   cheating on a paper or examination. This, for example, was
   the case among 42 percent of Amherst College students and
   30 percent of Johns Hopkins' undergraduates in 1974 (Peterson, 1974, p. 1; "Johns Hopkins Scraps Honor Code,"
   1975).

   With regard to theft and mutilation of library materials,
   a survey of college and university libraries found that mutilation of periodicals is a serious problem at 80 percent of the
   institutions studied (Hendrick and Murfin, 1974). The
   undergraduate libraries at the University of California,
   Berkeley; Northwestern University; and the University of
   Washington report annual loss rates between 4 and 5 percent
   of their collections. Even a 1 percent loss rate nationally
   would require 63.4 million dollars per year in replacement
   costs plus processing ("Light-Fingered Library Patrons Cost
   U.S. Taxpayers," 1976).
3. *Proliferating off-campus and out-of-state programs.* Such
   programs are growing quickly. For instance, in the 14 south-

ern states comprising the Southern Regional Education Board, 68 out-of-state institutions are offering programs. Thirty-nine of these institutions are operating in more than one state and two operate in all of them (Southern Regional Education Board, 1978). The president of the Council on Postsecondary Accreditation divides off-campus programs into three categories—(a) those that are diploma mills, (b) marginal schools dominated by "experiential education," and (c) "off-campus operations of accredited institutions where quality control varies from very good to very questionable" (Steif, 1978).

4. *Easy grades.* Between 1969 and 1976, the proportion of students with A and B grade-point averages rose from 35 percent to 59 percent and the proportion with averages of C or less declined from 25 percent to 13 percent (Carnegie Surveys, 1969-70; 1975-76). This is shown in the following table:

Grades	1969	1976
A, A+	2	8
A−	5	11
B+	11	18
B	17	22
B−	19	15
C+	23	15
C	18	10
C− and less	7	3

Note: Totals are more than 100 because of rounding.

Source: Carnegie Surveys, 1969-70; 1975-76.

5. *Admission of unqualified foreign students.* A 1977 College Board panel on international education found that American universities are eagerly pursuing foreign students, often without adequate review of their qualifications. Clifford F. Sjogren, Jr., chairman of the panel, charged " 'hucksterism' by some institutions and a fairly widespread tendency to admit foreign students who are unqualified because of declining

domestic enrollments" ("Colleges Warned of Danger in Admitting Foreign Students Who Lack Qualifications," 1977, p. 6). Indeed, foreign student enrollments rose by 13 percent in a single academic year—from 179,340 in 1976-77 to 203,070 in 1977-78. At two-year colleges, the proportion of foreign students increased from 10.6 percent of total enrollments in 1969, to 15.6 percent in 1976. The largest increase has come from wealthy underdeveloped nations. For instance, 25.6 percent of foreign students now come from OPEC nations ("203,068 Foreign Students Enroll at U.S. Colleges: 23,310 from Iran," 1978, p. 3).

6. *Inadequate support services.* This refers to services ranging from job placement to compensatory education to advising. For example, 27 percent of the undergraduates who have used academic advising, 27 percent of the undergraduates who have used personal advising, and 33 percent of the students who have used career advising rate it "inadequate" (Carnegie Surveys, 1975-76).

7. *Inaccurate or incomplete catalogs.* At least 81 percent of a representative sample of 1975 four-year college and university catalogs omitted one or more of the following types of information: (a) the type of instructor who teaches each course—graduate student or faculty; (b) the frequency with which courses are offered; (c) faculty status in terms of who is part-time, on-leave, and not teaching at the time the catalog is printed; (d) what high school courses are required for admission; (e) the forms of financial aid available and how to get them; and (f) the content of the courses listed (Catalog Study, 1976).

We are concerned about the prospective frantic search by many faculty members, many departments, and many colleges for scarce students in the 1980s and 1990s. Unless corrective actions are taken, such conditions are likely to lead some students to try to take even greater advantage of the situation, and to make some colleges even more reluctant to insist on ethical conduct by students and even more likely to engage in improper conduct themselves.

We are concerned that these negative behavioral traits may indicate a larger and more deep-seated problem: a general loss of self-confidence and of a sense of mutual trust, and a general decline in integrity of conduct on campus. The basic problem may be bigger than the sum of its component parts. "Rip-offs" and excessive "legalisms" are bad in themselves, but worse for what they imply about the general situation. One evidence of the latter is increased litigiousness (see Table 1). Already there

Table 1. Percentages of institutions reporting change in the number of lawsuits threatened or initiated by students, by Carnegie type

	Increased	*Remain the same*	*Decreased*
Research universities I	74	19	6
Research universities II	63	23	14
Doctorate-granting universities I	38	44	18
Doctorate-granting universities II	55	28	18
Comprehensive universities and colleges I	43	38	20
Comprehensive universities and colleges II	38	46	17
Liberal arts colleges I	34	63	4
Liberal arts colleges II	36	50	15
Two-year institutions	24	64	13
Average	35	51	14

Source: Carnegie Surveys, 1978.

has been clear erosion of public respect for some aspects of the conduct of some individuals and some institutions. This erosion of respect is one basis for erosion of support, and for the increasing and alarming loss of institutional autonomy. It does no good to deny bad practices when they exist. It does some good to acknowledge them and to seek to correct them.

Whether or not ethical conduct has deteriorated to a significant degree in some areas of campus activities, and we are convinced that in some ways it is clearly less defensible, we are concerned that there is more scrutiny of campus conduct by students, by the public, by the states, by the federal government, and by the press. As a consequence of this, it is at least prudent for a campus to give prior scrutiny to itself.

We present this report as an audit of the current situation. We also present it as a warning about what the future might possibly hold. In Section 4, we set forth our recommendations and checklists for students, for trustees of institutions, and for accrediting associations as a means of helping to improve conduct where it is now deficient. We do not recommend a greatly increased role for public authority, rather the contrary, but we do make several specific suggestions for further action. In Appendix A, we set forth sources of information about illustrative constructive actions by private and public authorities.

The improvements we suggest are mostly designed to reduce clear abuses in specific areas; we do not, regretfully, have solutions for whatever underlying problems there may be.

A period of intensified competition for students requires an intensified concern for rights and responsibilities within the academic community and their reasonable enforcement.

2

Institutional Rights and Student Responsibilities

This section of our report concerns the reciprocal rights and responsibilities of students and institutions with respect to academic programming, tuition and financial aid, and admissions. A great deal is known about some of these responsibilities, a little about others, and only the sensational aspects are known about a few. The intent of this section is to describe and give examples of general behavior patterns, not to document them in their entirety. It concludes with a discussion of recent enforcement efforts by students, institutions of higher education, and social policy agencies—the states, the federal government, and accrediting associations. Here again the goal is to describe the nature of the efforts of each group, not to catalog them in full.

Academic Programming

This is the portion of higher education most intimately concerned with teaching and learning; thus it is the core of the academic enterprise. Institutional rights and student responsibilities in this domain include:

1. Learning needs and desires should provide the rationale for enrolling in academic programs. Students should not manipulate programs to achieve other ends.
2. The learner should be informed. Catalogs and other institu-

tionally disseminated literature on academic programs should be read.

3. The learner should take an active part in planning and executing his or her academic program within the context of stated requirements and existing institutional resources.
4. The learner should continually monitor his or her academic progress.
5. The learner should seek out available academic support services such as basic skills instruction, job placement, and advising as needed.
6. The learner should attend class and participate in other learning activities, come prepared, and complete assignments on time.
7. The principle of academic honesty should be embraced.
8. The freedom of the academic community to inquire, publish, and teach should be respected.
9. The facilities and property of the academic community (for example, buildings, books, and computers) should also be respected.

One way to understand how well students are carrying out their responsibilities is to examine how and where they are slipping. Cheating and other forms of academic dishonesty were highly publicized in the aftermath of the West Point scandal. In a Spring 1974 Amherst College poll, "42 percent of the responding students said they had cheated on an exam or paper while at Amherst" (Peterson, 1974, p. 1). In the same year, a poll at Johns Hopkins, an institution which operated on the basis of an honor code, showed that "30 percent of the undergraduates had cheated in one way or another by their senior year" ("Johns Hopkins Scraps Honor Code," 1975). Nationally, 8.8 percent of the undergraduates responding to the 1976 Carnegie Council survey said some forms of cheating were necessary to get the grades they wanted. This represents an increase of 1.3 percentage points over 1969 (Carnegie Surveys, 1969-70; 1975-76). The variation among students in different types of colleges is shown in Table 2.

Some term paper companies are still in operation, but it is

Table 2. Percentages of students responding that "some forms of
cheating are necessary to get the grades I want,"
by Carnegie type in 1976 and 1969

	1976	1969
Research universities I	9.4	5.8
Research universities II	10.5	5.3
Doctorate-granting universities I	7.5	6.4
Doctorate-granting universities II	11.2	7.8
Comprehensive universities and colleges I	11.1	9.0
Comprehensive universities and colleges II	10.6	10.6
Liberal arts colleges I	6.0	3.9
Liberal arts colleges II	7.9	8.1
Two-year institutions	6.5	7.8
Average	8.8	7.5

Source: Carnegie Surveys, 1969-70; 1975-76.

impossible to guess how many students use them. Collegiate Research Systems, a major east coast company with three regional
offices and 6,000 papers in its files, estimates that "less than
one percent of college students in the country" take advantage
of the service ("Term Paper Companies Claim Persecution by
Academia, Seek Respectability," 1977, p. 2).

The theft and mutilation of library books is a problem on
most campuses. As noted in Section 1, a 1972 national survey
of college and university libraries found that mutilation of periodicals was a serious problem at 80 percent of the institutions
studied (Hendrick and Murfin, 1974). With regard to books, a
1976 library inventory at the Claremont Colleges found 15,000
volumes had been stolen over the last 20 years. At the University of Maryland more than 30,000 books were missing. Tufts
University reports that almost 8 percent of the books in its
library disappear after a year on the shelves. In 1976, Princeton
University found that articles on aspirin and its derivatives were
ripped out of more than 100 journals. And colleges and universities throughout the country have found that Winslow Homer
prints have been razored out of nineteenth century journals

("National Crime Wave Plagues University Libraries," 1976, p. 5). The undergraduate libraries at the University of California, Berkeley; Northwestern University; and University of Washington report annual book loss rates of between 4 and 5 percent of their holdings. At Berkeley, 12 percent of the 150,000 volume undergraduate collection was lost in three years with an average replacement cost of ten dollars plus processing cost per book. As a consequence, 10 percent of the library's annual budget was used for book replacement. And the editors of *Library Scene* estimate the national replacement cost of college and university libraries to be no less than 63.7 million dollars plus processing each year if only 1 percent of library collections are lost per year ("Light-Fingered Library Patrons Cost U.S. Taxpayers," 1976). Students are not the sole cause of this vandalism but certainly are contributors.

Stories about students altering their transcripts appear in newspapers from time to time ("Queens College Uncovers Grade Tampering Scheme," 1978, p. 2; Peterson, 1974, p. 1). At UCLA, for instance, three students were caught trying to change their grades by sneaking into the university's computer system (Magarrell, 1978, p. 1).

Computer dishonesty of this type is a relatively new phenomenon, but one that may be on the rise. For example, three University of Wisconsin students are alleged to have used a faculty member's computer time worth at least $300 for projects such as making Snoopy (Charles Schultz's dog) designs; a student at Wayne State learned the password for a university research project and charged $2,000 worth of computer time to it; and a California engineering student gained access to a Pacific Telephone and Telegraph Company inventory computer by using telephone beeper tones and managed to steal over $1 million worth of equipment before he was caught. To be sure, the number of students with the skill to engage in such activity is small (Magarrell, 1978, p. 1). Nonetheless this is an area where possibilities for abuse may be expected to increase in the future.

Some forms of academic manipulation may not be dishonest, but are certainly ethically dubious. Almost half (47 percent) of American college students believe that many successful students at their college make it by "beating the system" rather than by studying (Carnegie Surveys, 1975-76). Eighteen percent of the undergraduates responding to the 1976 Carnegie Council survey said that getting a degree was more important than the content of their courses. When ends are more important than means, one result is likely to be circumventive innovation designed to achieve the end (a degree) without having to go through the accepted means (taking courses) for getting there. Some people, who by definition are not students, turn to "easy degrees" or mail order degrees. They are served by organizations like the Diploma Service Company, which operates in at least New York and until recently California, and does a thriving business furnishing customers with "beautiful exacting copies" of diplomas from almost any college or university in the country for $10 and up ("For $45, You Can Buy a Fake Stanford Degree," 1978, p. 14).

Artificially hiking grade-point averages is more common. This involves such practices as overenrolling in courses and dropping those in which one is doing poorly on the last possible drop day; taking one or more courses pass/fail and working harder in graded courses (34 percent of undergraduates responding to the 1976 Carnegie Council survey who had taken pass-fail courses said they work harder in their graded courses); changing from pass/fail to letter or numerical grades in a course or vice versa after the first hourly examination; taking "gut courses," "Mickey Mouse courses," or highly-graded courses (which the *Brown Alumni News* reports is on the rise—"Whatever Happened to the 'C'?" 1975); and sabotaging a fellow student's work.

An alternative is simply "goofing off." Nineteen percent of 1976 college students, a 3 percentage point decrease since 1969, said they do not work hard in their courses (Carnegie Surveys, 1969-70; 1975-76). The penalties for doing this are less severe than in previous decades, owing to grade inflation, which will be discussed in the next section.

Many students have not tried to be informed, have not taken an active part in planning or monitoring their educations, or have failed to seek out needed support services. In a study of undergraduate curriculum at 26 colleges and universities, Levine and Weingart (1973, pp. 14, 129) reported that "substantial portions of the student body at each school said flatly they had no interest in using advisers regardless of the accessibility or knowledge of such advisers." Many students admitted that they contacted their adviser to get his or her signature only five minutes before semester programs were due. Practices such as forging the signature of an adviser were also noted. Levine and Weingart (1973, p. 129) concluded that "students were not aware of the curriculum opportunities available to them. When asked whether they had considered creating their own major, many were amazed that such a possibility existed, and substantial numbers of students at several schools supplied the interviewers with misinformation."

By now several important points should be clear. First, many students are not fully carrying out their responsibilities. Second, the most serious breaches of responsibility, such as academic dishonesty, usually involve relatively small numbers of students. Cheating on tests and papers is an unfortunate exception that appears to involve a substantial minority of undergraduates. Third, students themselves are the principal victims of many of their lapses of responsibility—not being informed, passivity in academic planning, and not using available institutional services when needed.

There has been some activity by colleges, students, and social policy agencies aimed at improving the situation; but institutional efforts have been spotty. Colleges and their faculties have generally tended to be lax in punishing students for academic dishonesty. In the case of computer crime, Magarrell (1978, p. 1) noted that some universities such as Wisconsin and Wayne State prosecute students; on many other campuses, however, such episodes "are often treated as pranks." Five of Boston's "Big 8" universities (Boston College, Harvard, University of Massachusetts, Massachusetts Institute of Technology, and Northeastern) took no action against students using or working for term paper companies, even after the students' names were obtained through litigation (Boffey, 1974, p. 1). New York colleges were told by the state's attorney general that if they did not crack down on term paper company users they might face state legal action ("Crack Down on Cheaters, New York Colleges Told," 1974, p. 8). And on cheating, Iver Peterson (1974, p. 1) wrote that, unlike West Point, "liberal arts colleges have been reluctant to deal harshly with cheaters. In most cases, credit for the course has been withdrawn or course grading dropped by a letter." He neglected to say that some faculty only require the cheating student to redo a paper or retake an examination. Possible rationales for this situation can be traced to the desperate enrollment straits of many colleges and fear of liability or lengthy legal entanglements on the part of some institutions and faculty.

This is not, of course, true of all institutions. Colgate and Columbia, among others, have taken a strong stance against plagiarism ("Crack Down on Cheaters, New York Colleges Told," 1974, p. 8). Others have taken deterrent steps. For instance, The Johns Hopkins University scrapped its 65-year-old honor code and approved monitors for examinations in the aftermath of student complaints of cheating ("Johns Hopkins Scraps Honor System," 1975); the University of California, Berkeley, is planning a change in its grading system to make it less subject to manipulation by adding to the typical college transcript mean course grades in classes with more than ten students (The Carnegie Foundation for the Advancement of Teaching, 1977); Wayne State University has instituted "mousetraps" and code words in its computer system to catch or discourage people from interfering with it (Magarrell, 1978, p. 1); the Claremont Colleges, rather than losing thousands of books a year, have instituted an electronic library security system, which, on an average, reduces library loss rates by 50 to 80 percent and generally pays for itself within three years ("National Crime Wave Plagues University Libraries," 1976, p. 5); and West Point has added "a series of courses in morals and ethics to its curriculum" ("Ethics Courses Added to West Point Curriculum," 1978, p. 21).

Students, by and large, have been unwilling to blow the whistle on peers who cheat. For example, a 1974 survey at the University of California, Davis, found that 75.4 percent of the respondents would not report another student they observed cheating to the judicial board (Bow, 1975). Yet most students want those found guilty of serious dishonesty to receive an appropriate penalty. For instance, when a Harvard student who stole literally thousands of books from the university's library was given a relatively light penalty by the Administrative Board of the graduate school, students complained and the *Harvard Crimson* published an outraged editorial.

More tangible efforts by students are numerous, but generally restricted to individual campuses. Exemplary of these are the student resource center at Brown University, which reaches out to students to tell them about curricular options, available campus services, and how to use them. An exception to the individual campus pattern is the work of the National Student Educational Fund in Washington, D.C. Supported by the Fund for the Improvement of Postsecondary Education, it runs an annual contest to choose the best efforts by students to better inform other students.

Social policy traditionally has not been involved in this area because matters of institutional rights and student responsibility in academic affairs have been regarded as the prerogative of the higher education community. However, when student irresponsibility has moved into the realm of fraud and theft, social agencies have become more active. A hands-off attitude still lingers, though, in part because most student responsibilities are not subject to legislative enforcement. There are exceptions. For instance, at least five states—Massachusetts, Maryland, Illinois, Pennsylvania, and New York—have taken tough stands to deal with term paper sales. A Massachusetts law affects both the buyer and the seller. Sale of term papers and the use of "ringers" for examinations are prohibited with a maximum penalty set at a $100 fine and six months in prison. A Maryland law was aimed at sellers, but the future of such legislation is doubtful, because the Baltimore County Circuit Court overturned Maryland's law for violating the free speech provisions of the United States Constitution ("Maryland Term-Paper Ban Ruled Unconstitutional," 1975, p. 2). And California, in response to recent exposes on the Diploma Service Corporation, passed a law making it a misdemeanor to print or sell copies of a college's diploma without its board's approval ("California Law Bars Diploma-Sales Companies," 1978, p. 2).

Another example of social policy involvement at the federal level is legislation to control computer crime that is currently being considered. Outlawed practices would include: (1) "introduction of fraudulent records or data into a computer system"; (2) "unauthorized use of computer facilities"; (3) "alteration or distruction of information in files"; and (4) "stealing, by electronic means or otherwise, of money, financial instruments, property, services, or valuable data" (Magarrell, 1978, p. 1).

Financial Aid and Tuition

For many students, financial aid and tuition are the key to college access and a source of growing influence in the world of higher education. For institutions, financial aid and tuition are essential for survival. Institutional rights and student responsibilities in this area include:

1. Students and potential students should be informed. They should be knowledgeable about the full cost of education, available financial aid programs and obligations, refund policies, and the financial stability at their college or the colleges they are thinking of applying to. Toward this end, all students should read institutional statements on tuition and fees, and those students who want financial assistance should read institutional statements on that subject and consult the financial aid office.
2. The rationale for seeking financial aid should be to meet the costs of an education that could not be met, or could be met only with hardship, in the absence of such aid. Education should not be used as a vehicle for securing financial aid.
3. Students should read and fully comprehend contracts before signing them.
4. Tuition and financial aid reporting should be complete and accurate.

5. Tuition and financial aid obligations should be satisfied in a timely fashion.

Students have not completely fulfilled these responsibilities and the failings have been the subject of heavy press coverage—particularly student loan defaults or other violations of tuition or financial aid responsibility number 5. About one out of every eight loans made under the Guaranteed Student Loan (GSL) program was not repaid after graduation or leaving school ("HEW to Step Up Collection of Direct Loans," 1978, p. 3). Seventeen percent of National Direct Student Loan (NDSL) recipients have also defaulted. The rate varies significantly at different types of institutions as shown in Table 3 (U.S. Office

Table 3. Percentages of National Direct Student Loans in default
at different types of institutions

Public universities	16
Public four-year colleges	18
Public two-year colleges	33
Private universities	14
Private four-year colleges	16
Private two-year colleges	23
Vocational institutions	32
Proprietary schools	30
Average	17

Source: U.S. Office of Education, 1978.

of Education, 1978). The rate of Veterans Administration education loan nonrepayment ran 44 percent as of December 31, 1977. However, these are high risk loans available only to people who have been denied other types of assistance. They are few in number and defaults are under 3,000 ("VA Education Loans Hit 44 Percent Default Rate, GAO Reports," 1978, p. 1). Finally, a relatively small percent of students have legally discharged their defaulted loans by declaring bankruptcy—by 1978 1,600 Guaranteed Student Loan borrowers and 20,245 National

Direct Student Loan recipients had filed for bankruptcy ("Senate Panel Clears Ban on Student Loan Bankruptcies," 1978, p. 3).

There has also been some inaccurate reporting and use of education as a mechanism to secure financial aid. The Veterans Administration attributes 41 percent of nearly 1.4 billion dollars in ex-GI overpayments to schools and veterans failing to report such academic changes as dropping courses or withdrawing from school ("VA Proposes Rules for Processing School Liability Cases," 1978, pp. 3-4). The Basic Educational Opportunity Grant (BEOG) is estimated to have overpaid students $150 million since its inception six years ago ("OE Planning Changes in BEOG Validation Procedures for Colleges," 1978, p. 5). Contributing to this situation has been the manipulation of financial aid programs. At a community college studied by Harvey London (1978), it was found that veterans and others would drop in and register to pick up some temporarily needed money and then drop out. Overenrolling in courses and dropping some at the end of the term is another way to accomplish the same purpose. Unfortunately colleges sometimes hire extra faculty to teach these vanishing surplus students.

There have also been a small number of cases of alleged forgery and other criminal offenses. One of the largest involved 106 Pennsylvania students ("PA Arrests Students on Loan-Fraud Charges," 1976, p. 2).

Student financial aid abuse of this type is a serious problem, but the relative number of students involved is small. There were over 11 million people enrolled in higher education in 1976-77; however, only 695,000 received GSL funds and 751,000 received NDSL monies (U.S. National Center for Education Statistics, 1978; Atelsek and Gomberg, 1977, p. 14), and our data shows that fewer than one-fifth of the recipients are guilty of loan abuses. The fact of the matter is that the most common violation of responsibility among college students is failure to be informed about financial aid and tuition matters as well as signing forms without understanding the obligations they entail. This may be an even greater cause for default than deliberate dishonesty.

A number of remedies are currently being attempted. Social policy agencies, particularly at the federal executive and legislative level, have been the most active. Until the glare of the public eye fell upon loan cheating and defaults, the U.S. Office of Education which administers the GSL, NDSL, and BEOG programs was not, according to the Government Accounting Office, "aggressive" in trying to collect repayments or in bringing delinquent cases to court (Roark, 1977). However, there has recently been a flurry of activity at the Office of Education. Health, Education, and Welfare Secretary Califano announced measures to reduce NDSL defaults including institutional financial aid staff workshops, "due diligence" procedures that institutions will be required to observe, site inspections of institutions which do not practice "due diligence," and proposed legislation to allow the Internal Revenue Service to keep track of defaulted borrowers. With regard to GSL, the adequacy of institutional administrative and financial standards will be reviewed before colleges are allowed to participate, and already participating institutions will be reviewed every three years. Efforts to collect loans will also be more aggressive ("HEW Tightens Control Over Student Aid Programs," 1978, p. 2; "HEW to Extend Checks for GSL Defaulters to Military Personnel," 1978, p. 4). And initial reports indicate that these techniques are increasing loan repayments ("HEW to Step Up Collection of Direct Loans," 1978, p. 3).

With regard to basic grants (BEOGs), new regulations require institutions to verify several types of application data, not to give BEOGs to students who owe refunds to federal aid programs, and to establish standards for satisfactory academic progress in order to continue participating. In addition, the regulations prohibit student federal loan defaulters from receiving BEOG aid and formalize procedures for dropping institutions from the program ("OE Proposes New BEOG Regulations to Clarify Procedures, Clamp Down on Cheaters," 1978, p. 4; "OE Planning Changes in BEOG Validation Procedures for Colleges," 1978). As a consequence of the new standards, the Office of Education is rejecting three times as many student BEOG applicants this year as last ("OE Rejecting Three Times as Many

BEOG Applications This Year," 1978, p. 1). However, institutional spokespersons have criticized the procedures for being "complicated, time consuming, and likely to overload administrators and cause awards to be inequitably distributed" ("OE Planning Changes in BEOG Validation Procedures for Colleges," 1978, p. 5). And students are concerned about a possible "jam up" and delays in receiving aid ("OE Rejecting Three Times as Many BEOG Applications This Year," 1978, p. 1).

The Veterans Administration (VA) began making such changes earlier than the Office of Education did. However, a recent General Accounting Office report charged the high VA education loan default rate to the agency's "glaring failure to adequately review loan applications and follow-up on borrowers" ("VA Education Loans Hit 44 Percent Default Rate, GAO Reports," 1978, p. 1).

In Congress two additional pieces of legislation are of note. The first is now a law which bars ex-students from declaring bankruptcy to discharge themselves of their federal education loans. And the second is legislation introduced by Representative Ronald Mottl which would allow the Internal Revenue Service to turn over to HEW addresses of Guaranteed and National Direct Student Loan defaulters.

The courts have made several important rulings affecting bankruptcy. In the case of *Girdier* v. *Webster College* (1977), the Eighth Circuit U.S. Court of Appeals ruled that a college—public or private—may withold transcripts from students who have discharged their student loans through bankruptcy ("Court Says No Transcripts for Bankrupt Student Debtors," 1977, p. 5). And in another 1977 case, the New York State Court of Appeals overturned two lower court rulings and found a student could not go into bankruptcy to avoid repaying education loans. The student, W. G. Wilkes, who declared bankruptcy after graduating from college in 1970, having financed his education with NDSL, had little in the way of other debts and was gainfully employed at $9,000 a year with the state education department ("Student Bankruptcies Rejected by New York Judges," 1977, p. 6).

Activity at the state level has not been particularly significant, nor widespread. However, there have been noteworthy actions. For example, in 1977 Pennsylvania enacted a law permitting the garnishment of the salaries of defaulters working for the state. Several states, particularly New York, have followed suit by adopting similar laws or tracking down defaulters ("State Agencies Tracking Down Employees with Defaulted Loans," 1978, p. 5). Another tactic taken by New York State was to tighten the definition of student "emancipation" for purposes of receiving aid. Students must "submit additional proof" that they no longer receive financial support from parents ("New York Tightens 'Emancipated Student' Definition," 1976).

The most notable efforts by students and institutions have been in encouraging students to be better informed. This will be discussed in the next section.

Admissions

Today the attention in admissions is on student rights; however, students also shoulder certain basic responsibilities and institutions are entitled to enjoy certain fundamental rights. These include:

1. Applicants and potential applicants should be knowledgeable about the available postsecondary opportunities and the colleges they are thinking of attending. With regard to potential colleges, both the information an institution publishes about itself and comparative and evaluative guides published outside the college should be read. Where possible, applicants should visit institutions and speak with students and faculty. When that is not possible, applicants should contact present or former students. When at all in doubt, they should call their state department of education and/or accrediting associations.
2. Applicants should honestly represent themselves in applying to a college.

Students are not delivering on responsibility number 1. Anyone who has talked with undergraduates is aware that most are knowledgeable neither about the opportunities available to them, nor about the colleges they plan to attend. In fact, some students resist learning about them. One rationale is fear. Students, particularly first generation nontraditional students, with exceptional ability or unique interests, who live in a one-college area, usually containing a two-year institution, are frequently unwilling to apply elsewhere even when told the local college cannot accommodate their needs, because they are afraid to venture away from familiar turf. Another rationale is the particularlistic choice of a college. For instance, a Carnegie Council staff member interviewed a student who wanted desperately to go to Harvard because his family had. He was rejected there but attended an excellent and prestigious college with a program as good or better than Harvard's in his area of interest. Nonetheless the young man could not be persuaded that the institution he was attending was a respectable one or that he need not reapply to Harvard.

Responsibility number 2 is neglected in small ways, consciously or unconsciously, by many college applicants, particularly those applying to selective programs or colleges. It happens when the potential student writes a required admissions essay or conducts a campus visit in a manner designed to conform to projected institutional standards rather than reflecting the applicant's true feelings. It also happens when friends or relatives write an applicant's required admissions essays. The consequences can be quite damaging for the applicant who guesses wrong about what an institution is looking for. A case in point is a student who wanted to attend an experimental subunit at a large state university—so she could design her own major. Her first application was rejected owing to size limitations, but she was encouraged to reapply. At that point the student decided her application had not been sufficiently radical for the college. She was rejected a second time. Her third application mentioned experiments with marijuana and LSD. It is not clear that she used the drugs, but in any case this was not what the college was looking for. They wanted students who were interested in forming their own programs. She was never admitted.

Gross misrepresentation is rare, but it does happen. We have all read newspaper stories about students who falsified a transcript and/or recommendations.

The repercussions of students' sloughing off admissions

responsibilities are often innocuous, but when they are negative it is usually the student who is the victim for the reasons already noted. But colleges can also suffer because of unwarranted and costly attrition of students who chose the wrong school and could easily have avoided it. Gross student misrepresentation is, of course, an exception. It abuses both institutions and fellow students. Colleges on the whole have treated this problem lightly as they have other forms of academic dishonesty.

As to remedies for the lesser problems, there is really little that can be done. Colleges and universities, students, and social policy have been inactive here. What is being done to encourage students to accept greater responsibility pertains more directly to student rights and will be discussed in the next section.

3

Student Rights and Institutional Responsibilities

Whereas the last section examined how well students were carrying out their responsibilities, this one is concerned with how well institutions are doing. Again the enforcement activities of colleges and universities, students, and social policy are reviewed.

Academic Programming

There are 16 basic rights and responsibilities associated with academic programming:

1. The emphasis in academic programming should be on quality.
2. Credit should be awarded where and only where credit is due.
3. Clear and specific written documents describing policies for accepting credit from other institutions should be available.
4. Accurate information on the possible acceptability of an institution's credits elsewhere should be disclosed.
5. Academic evaluation should be fair and reasonable. Grades and evaluations should be meaningful, timely, and based wholly on academic considerations. Transcripts or records of grades should be properly maintained. Confidentiality and access to records should be guaranteed in accordance with the 1974 Family Educational Rights and Privacy Act.

6. Academic degrees should be awarded when they are academically merited. Students should be informed regularly of their academic progress and should receive degrees after satisfying all stated academic requirements.
7. Adequate facilities and services to support academic programs should be provided.
8. Quality instruction should be offered. This includes faculty with appropriate training, faculty who teach in an area of expertise, faculty who keep up to date with their fields, faculty who meet scheduled classes, faculty who come to class prepared, faculty who are available to students outside of class, and in general, good teaching.
9. Institutional program requirements should be described in clear, specific, and accurate terms and should be available in written form. All requirements should be educationally meaningful.
10. Students should be notified of unusual features of academic programs that cannot be readily anticipated, such as an undergraduate biology department specializing in developmental biology rather than the general field.
11. Requirements should not be unconditionally changed for students who have already enrolled in a program.
12. Courses that are offered should be comparable to their catalog descriptions.
13. All courses listed in the catalog should be offered periodically.
14. All academic programs should be continued until enrolled students making acceptable progress have had an opportunity to graduate. Program changes should be well planned and widely communicated and should incorporate an orderly transition from the old to the new.
15. The principle of academic honesty should be embraced.
16. Causes for dismissal should be published in clear and specific form; students should be dismissed only for appropriate cause, and after due process.

We know a great deal about how colleges are carrying out some of these responsibilities and a little bit about the publicized aspects of several. Grade inflation is a problem throughout the country. Seventy-seven percent of the cross-section of American faculty responding to the 1975 Carnegie Council on Policy Studies in Higher Education survey felt it was becoming a serious problem. Sixty-one percent of the undergraduates responding to the same survey belived it was possible to get good grades without really understanding the material. Between 1969 and 1976, the proportion of students with A and B grade-point averages rose from 35 percent to 59 percent, and the proportion with averages of C or less dropped from 25 percent to 13 percent (Carnegie Surveys, 1969-70; 1975-76). During the same period Scholastic Aptitude Test scores and student competence in basic skills declined.

At some institutions credits are being awarded more liberally than in previous years. With the growing acceptance of nontraditional education, credit for off-campus learning (for example, experiential education, fieldwork, self-study, television instruction, and newspaper courses), and credit for prior learning or previous life experience are spreading to more and more college curricula. The former is granted by 63 percent of two-year and 82 percent of four-year arts and sciences colleges and the latter by 22 percent of the two-year and 32 percent of the four-year arts and sciences colleges (Catalog Study, 1976). At nontraditional institutions which have been working with these techniques longest, such as Metropolitan State University in Saint Paul, methods for assessing the award of credit are still experimental. At a number of other schools, the results have been somewhat haphazard. There is a temptation on the part of some colleges to adopt nontraditional techniques without adequate planning in order to compete with neighboring schools. For example, the recently revamped College Level Examination Program (CLEP), accepted for credit at 91 percent of four-year colleges and 86 percent of two-year institutions, was criticized in the past for being an easy source of credits (Levine, 1978, pp. 213, 215-216). When Utah State University gave three of the CLEP general examinations, each considered the equivalent of a one-year college introductory course, to 500 entering freshmen, 61 percent received credit in social science-history, 68 percent received credit in the humanities, and 77 percent received credit in the natural sciences. When San Francisco State University administered all five of the general examinations to two thirds of its entering freshmen, 38 percent became "instant sophomores," 72 percent received at least one semester of college credit, and 94 percent were granted at least six hours of college credit (Stecher, 1977, p. 36).

We also know that there are still a few mail order degree sellers and degree mills, thanks to the reporting of the "60 Minutes" staff (August 28, 1978) and John Bear's book *College Degrees by Mail: A Comprehensive Guide to Nontraditional Programs* (1978), which lists in its chapter on "Degree Mills and Diploma Mills" 37 institutions, some of which have deceptively legitimate sounding names such as Dallas State College, Jackson State College, and Western Reserve Education Service. In addition, the state of Illinois recently enjoined Great Lakes University from sales or advertising and charged its operator, who also ran a degree mill in Washington—Pacific Northwest University— with fraud. Great Lakes sold transcripts and degrees without classes, studying, or examinations, by mail through a Chicago mail drop ("Degree-Mill Operator Charged in Illinois," 1978, p. 2).

A number of university faculty are not available to students outside of class. For instance, 16 percent of faculty at the most research-oriented universities have no office hours (Carnegie Surveys, 1975-76). And instruction is not all it could or should be in some cases. Thirteen percent of undergraduates are dissatisfied or very dissatisfied with the teaching they have had at college, 27 percent of students who have used academic advising rate it "not very adequate," and 43 percent of students believe most faculty at their school are not strongly interested in the problems of undergraduates (Carnegie Surveys, 1975-76). In a study of eight regionally accredited degree-granting colleges, Jung and others (1976) surveyed 5,561 enrolled students. Three percent said that within the previous 12 months their instructor was changed at least twice after a course began and 22 percent said they were required to use outdated or worn-out equipment or facilities in at least a few classes.

There are weak programs even in some well-known universities. An example, prior to its reorganization, was the doctoral program in the Graduate School of Management at Vanderbilt University, which a Tennessee court ruled not only to be inadequate, but "hastily embarked on, vague, [and] ill defined" in the case of *Lowenthal* v. *Vanderbilt University* ("Vanderbilt Ordered to Pay Former Doctoral Students," 1977). As to other institutions, expert review panels have given low grades to 26 doctoral programs in the state of New York (Winkler, 1977) and 18 doctoral programs in Louisiana (Winkler, 1976). Requirements are still occasionally imposed or disposed of for noneducational reasons. At several institutions department chairpersons who opposed general education requirements a few years ago are now supportive because general education is a way for overstaffed departments, underenrolled faculty, and unemployed graduate assistants to find students to teach. On accepting transfer credit, Kintzer (1973) reports that some senior colleges insist on exact equivalence in the courses they accept from other schools, and everyone had heard horror stories of people who transferred and lost an unanticipated number of their previously earned credits.

A number of conditions—liberal grading, excessive credit for life experience, inadequate curricula, and use of nonuniversity faculty—have been found in combination in several off-campus programs run by profit-making companies under the aegis of well-known colleges. At least 11 universities in California offer programs through such companies (Watkins, 1977). And the New York State Regents recently completed a pilot study of the off-campus centers operated by 18 parent institutions in Westchester County. The Regents' consultant concluded that the programs were in general "academically deficient" ("Education Centers in New York Called Academically Deficient," 1978).

> "Throughout the programs failed to meet standards."
> Almost without exception, she said, the centers had
> no full-time faculty of their own, and instructors
> were often marginal in qualifications. There were no

libraries "in any conventional sense," the range of courses offered was narrow, and none of the centers operating in 1976 required a thesis for the master's degree ["Extensive Critique of Extensions," 1976].

The extension center is a growing phenomenon. A study by the Southern Regional Education Board (SREB) found 68 out-of-state institutions offering programs in the 14 SREB member states, 39 institutions were operating in more than one of the states, and two, University of La Verne and Upper Iowa State University, were operating in all of them. About these centers, SREB reported:

> The range of offerings is considerable, although technical, business administration, public administration and teacher education programs are among the most common. Some institutions . . . operate primarily on military bases and offer courses and programs to servicemen and women and their dependents (Pepperdine University, University of Southern California, Embry-Riddle Aeronautical University). Others specialize in teacher education, contracting with local school districts to provide courses and programs (University of La Verne, Rocky Mountain College). The University of Oklahoma offers master's programs in public administration and business administration. The Center for Degree Studies of Scranton, Pennsylvania offers a number of associate degree programs in engineering and electronic technologies. Drew University of New Jersey offers a doctorate in theology.
> Programs operating out-of-state often employ local coordinators who contract with community resource people and faculty members from other institutions to teach courses in local high schools, community or military base facilities, federal office buildings, or hotel meeting rooms. In some cases, the out-of-state programs have more extensive facilities resembling those of a "branch" or off-campus center.

On military bases, faculty sometimes teach for more than one institution, and registrars or admissions officers are employed by more than one institution at the same time [Southern Regional Education Board, 1978].

There is no evidence of widespread abrogation of academic program responsibilities by colleges and universities, but there is some neglect even in a few well-respected institutions. Off-campus centers are a special case. They combine both innovative nontraditional programs and fly-by-night operations, representing vendorism at its best and worst. Kenneth Young, president of the Council on Postsecondary Accreditation, divides them into three categories:

- Those that are clearly "diploma mills."
- Marginal schools dominated by "experiential learning." He cited a school that was asked by a middle-aged woman for degree credit for writing a paper about her abortion experience.
- The "off-campus operations of accredited institutions where quality control varies from very good to very questionable" [in Steif, July 10, 1978, p. 9].

The management of academic programs has traditionally been considered the purview of colleges and universities, and social policy has stayed generally outside this realm. However, this is no longer the case. The courts, in particular, have been moving further and further into the classroom. They have ruled on the most fundamental matters—course and program quality and content—in cases such as *Lowenthal* v. *Vanderbilt University,* which was already discussed, and *Ianello* v. *The University of Bridgeport,* in which a student complained that a required course did not match the university catalog description, lacked tests or grades, was of minimal substance, and failed to provide a useful critique of her work. Unlike the Vanderbilt students, Ianello lost, not on the grounds that the court lacked expertise to judge such matters, but because she failed to prove her case.

State and federal statutes and regulations are increasing in this area, but they tend to be spotty in their coverage and far less intrusive than the courts. At the state level, the majority of states have rather general statutes or regulations of generally vague or undemanding character for public degree-granting institutions pertaining to curriculum and faculty qualifications. For private degree-granting institutions, 40 percent of the states have licensing and oversight statutes and regulations dealing with course length, content, goals, or objectives; 50 percent on faculty qualifications; 38 percent on degrees, diplomas, credentials or graduate requirements; and 46 percent on facility standards. The most frequent recent additions to state law have been in the area of controlling off-campus and external degree programs (Jung and others, 1977).

At the federal level, the few academic program regulations are rather new and have been tied to participation in federal financial aid programs. The Veterans Administration, for example, will not accept approval for programs which are less than two years old, which enroll students in a class consisting of 85 percent or more federally supported members, or which do not meet certain credit requirements. These requirements, which can be waived, are intended to avoid abuses such as those noted earlier in some off-campus centers. However, they have been criticized for intruding into substantive academic policy.

Academic program review has been a feature of the work of the accrediting associations for a long time, but concern with the practices discussed previously appears to be on the rise in the written statements of a number of the regional associations and the Council on Postsecondary Accreditation (COPA), the national coordinating body. On the subject of off-campus centers, COPA reported "mounting evidence of inferior off-campus programs" and asked the regional associations to develop suitable policies to deal with them. Despite some foot dragging, all of the regionals now have some policy or other. Most, though not all, require members to notify them 90 days in advance of new off-campus programs and await approval.

Institutional Advertising

Advertising is the first contact many students have with a college and the only contact some students have before enrolling. Here student rights and institutional responsibilities are four:

1. Advertising should be accurate and reliable.
2. Advertising should be up to date.
3. Advertising should be complete—balanced and comprehensive.
4. Advertising should be understandable.

The earliest college advertising we know of is a 1643 Harvard promotional tract entitled "New England's First Fruit." Though reflective of what parents wanted from college three-and-a-half centuries ago, it has all the charm today of an invitation to attend reform school. In five pages, it does, however, discuss Harvard's history and purpose, the college's facilities, its staff, the requirements for admission, student responsibilities and institutional rules, the academic schedule, and graduation requirements.

Times have changed and higher education's new missions, enormous growth in scale, adoption of the course system, and acceptance of the elective curriculum have necessitated new forms of advertising. Last year, the Iowa Regents voted to allow its universities to advertise via radio and television ("Iowa Regents Will Allow Universities to Advertise," 1977). Other colleges are turning to disposable 45 RPM records, slide shows, newspaper and magazine ads, view books, and college fairs. But the college catalog is the best known and most maligned advertisement of all.

A 1963 study by Elton and Donohew reported that high school guidance counselors did not believe they could rely on college catalogs for accurate information, and a 1969 doctoral dissertation by John Speegle found major discrepencies between the catalog descriptions of eight colleges and the perceptions of the colleges by enrolled upperclassmen (Stark, 1976, p. 60).

Institutions face an unavoidable tension between using the

catalog to define the relationship between themselves and their students and using the catalog as an instrument to attract prospective students. Painting a school in too positive a light makes a catalog inaccurate and unreliable; so does inadvertantly including in a catalog out-of-date information, courses that are no longer offered, course descriptions that differ from the substance of the courses actually given, pictures of undergraduates working with scientific equipment that is not ordinarily available to them, suggestions that a program will lead to employment, photographs of students in small seminars or a student and teacher casually talking when freshmen are unlikely to enjoy such experiences, or several pictures of minority events when an institution has only a very few minority students.

Another catalog problem is incomplete information. A Carnegie Council staff study of 1975 catalogs from 210 representative four-year colleges and universities found that:

- 81 percent of the catalogs did not list the instructors of their courses
- 72 percent of the catalogs did not tell when their courses would next be offered or how frequently the courses were given
- 56 percent of the catalogs did not tell any one of the following—which faculty were part-time, which were on leave, and which were not teaching
- 18 percent of the catalogs neither explained which, if any, high school courses were required for admission, nor directed interested parties to another source for that information
- 17 percent of the catalogs neither explained what types of financial aid were available and how to get them, nor directed interested parties to another source for that information (a sizeable number of institutions had not updated their catalogs to include Basic Educational Opportunity Grants despite the fact that they had been available since 1973)
- 5 percent of the catalogs did not describe the content of the courses listed

At any institution which omits time schedules for courses,

faculty teaching status, and high school course requirements, it is possible for the entering student to expect all courses to be available each year, all faculty to be teaching undergraduates, all courses to be taught by faculty, and no high school courses to be required.

The catalog study shows that many colleges and universities are not completely fulfilling their advertising responsibilities to students. But the evidence does not indicate that institutions of higher education are intentionally abusing students' rights or that advertising is intentionally misleading. Moreover, some institutions have recently taken steps to alleviate the problem noted.

The Fund for the Improvement of Postsecondary Education's (FIPSE) "Better Information for Student Choice" project is probably the most interesting development on campus in this matter. Eleven pilot institutions (University of California, Los Angeles; University of California, Irvine; Portland State University; Barat College; Morris Brown College; University of Illinois, Urbana-Champaign; Monroe Community College; Macomb County Community College; Mountain Empire Community College; Heald Business College; and National Radio Institute) were given support to produce a prospectus or consumer-oriented catalog. FIPSE borrowed the term "prospectus" from the Securities Exchange Commission, "which requires that a corporation offering stock to the public first publish a verified prospectus, disclosing the facts deemed relevant for an informed decision to buy that stock" (Marchese, 1976). Each of the 11 project colleges took a different approach to the catalogs, but included "such things as current regional and national information on the availability of jobs by career field; accurate educational cost projections; descriptions and explanations of student attrition and retention rates; types of students who are most productive at the institution; current student and faculty perceptions of the quality of the learning process [for instance, the Barat College prospectus rates the suitability of its departments for majors] and student-faculty interactions; the environment of the institution as viewed by various subcultures; and the assessment by graduates of the relationship between the educational experience and job requirements" (Fund for the Improvement of Postsecondary Education, 1976, p. 149).

The Barat College prospectus, considered one of the most successful products of the Better Information Project, contained the contents shown in Table 4. It cost $30,000 to create and publish. And Ted Marchese who directed the Barat project believes the long run difference in cost between it and a college's usual catalog to be minimal. The cost for the first year's prospectus is, however, considerably more than that of subsequent years.

To supplement the work of the individual colleges, FIPSE also established a Better Information task force under the auspices of the Education Commission of the States, which explored the following questions: "Why better information; which types of information are helpful and why; what information can be provided responsibly and how; what are the process issues in prospectus building; does form of communication make a difference; what are the possibilities for determining the effectiveness of better information and for determining its validity; can better information be provided in order that prospective students might make comparisons among institutions; and what are the varying institutional impacts relative to voluntary versus mandated disclosure of information" (Fund for the Improvement of Postsecondary Education, 1976, p. 149). The work of the National Task Force on Better Information for Student Choice has resulted in numerous publications, such as *Better Information for Student Choice: Report of a National Task Force* (1978) on how to produce high-information catalogs.

The idea of a catalog audit was another product of the task force. Both the University of California, Irvine, and the Barat College FIPSE teams involved large numbers of faculty and students in reviewing their prospectuses. Though this procedure may not seem noteworthy, it is a departure from the practices of most colleges where the catalog is primarily the responsibility of the admissions and publication offices (Stark and Marchese, 1978). However, Barat went even a step further and brought an external team onto campus to evaluate the accuracy of its catalog.

A course of action taken by some other colleges, including Florida State University, is simply to place a disclaimer in the front of their old catalog stating that it is subject to change. The legality of this technique has not yet been tested.

Governmental actions regarding the college catalog have been significant, though not at the state legislative and executive level. Few states have statutes or regulations regarding the content of the catalogs in public degree-granting institutions and only 14 have them for private colleges, though as many as 10 others require certain types of information to be available, published, or furnished prior to enrollment. Oregon has perhaps the most rigorous state law governing the public sector: "Advertising and publicity on behalf of public higher education are functions reserved for the Department of Higher Education and are to be released under the Department's name. Any advertising or publicity must present the prospects for employment in the fields of study" (Jung and others, 1977, p. 71).

At the federal level, legislative and executive policy is more rigorous. In part owing to high student guaranteed loan default rates and lack of state action, Congress and the departments concerned with education have become increasingly involved in matters relating to catalogs and promise to extend their involvement. The Education Amendments of 1976 contained a provision on "Student Consumer Information Services," which requires institutions participating in certain federal student aid programs to provide students and prospective students who request it with (1) a description of all financial aids—federal, state, and institutional—available to students who enroll at the college, including their requirements, means of applying, criteria for selection, and criteria for determining the amount of awards; (2) statements of the rights and responsibilities of students receiving federal financial aid, criteria for continued eligibility, criteria for determining that a student is in good academic standing and maintaining satisfactory progress in his course of study, the means by which aid payments will be made and their frequency, the terms of any loans, and repayment schedules for sample loans; (3) an accounting and explanation of the full costs of attending college; (4) a statement of institu-

Table 4. Contents of the Barat College Prospectus

Introduction	Page

What Is a Prospectus?

A new, experimental way of presenting the complete and accurate information you need to choose a college.

2

Key Facts at a Glance

Twenty-four pieces of information about Barat.

3

A Tradition of Educating Women

A short history of the college. After 176 years, Madeleine Sophie Barat's concept of humanizing education still makes sense for contemporary women.

4

How Barat Sees Itself

An interview with the President: "Years ago, some students were sent here for social prestige; now people make their own choice to come, for an education."

5

Academic Life at Barat	Page

How the Curriculum Works

"largely elective....all work planned on an individual basis with the help of an advisor."

6

Options for Students

...on campus, in Chicago, and abroad, plus information on independent study, developing skills, planning a career, and other matters.

7

Patterns of Study

Course offerings, class size, teaching styles, work load, and advisement, and what students say about them.

8

Thumbnail Sketches

Statistical and impressionistic views of 18 departments and the majors they offer.

11

Who Teaches at Barat?

"The college employs and promotes teachers primarily on the basis of their demonstrated effectiveness in teaching."

12

How Good is the Library?

In an interview, the librarian describes its strengths and weaknesses.

13

A Climate for Learning

Lectures, concerts, and plays; campus and Chicago-area resources described and evaluated.

14

tional refund policies; (5) a description of the institution's academic program including degree and nondegree programs, related facilities, and all instructional staff; (6) data regarding student retention; and (7) if available, information on the number and percentage of students completing the program in which the inquirer is interested. The Guaranteed Student Loan program also requires information on placement rates.

Most federal agencies do not regulate the content of catalogs, though at least two, the Veterans Administration (VA) and the Federal Trade Commission (FTC), which deals so far only with proprietary schools, have their own requirements for institutional disclosure which are somewhat different from provisions of the Education Amendments of 1976 administered by the U.S. Office of Education. For schools to participate in VA programs, for instance, their catalogs, which are required to contain information varying from course outlines to transfer credit policy, must be formally certified as "true and correct." In addition, the Internal Revenue Service, the Postal Service, the Department of Justice, the Office of Civil Rights, and the 1974 Family Educational Rights and Privacy Act have requirements for public disclosure of specific types of information that must be or are generally satisfied by inclusion in the college catalog (Federal Interagency Committee on Education, 1978). As a supplement to these federal actions, several accrediting associations, private organizations and task forces, and researchers in the field of consumerism have also drawn up lists of what institutional catalogs should contain.

However, the most dramatic catalog developments have occurred in the courts, which are holding in increasing numbers of decisions that the catalog represents a contract between the student and his or her college.[1] This position is by no means

[1]The character of the contract can and has been variously constructed. Its uniqueness is highlighted in the appellate court opinion of *Slaughter* v. *Brigham Young University* (1975). "It is apparent that some elements of the law of contracts are used and should be used in the analysis of the relationship between plaintiff and the university to provide some framework into which to put the problem of expulsion for disciplinary reasons. This does not mean that 'contract law' must be rigidly applied in all its aspects, nor is it so applied even when the contract analogy is extensively adopted. The student-university relationship is unique and it should not and cannot be stuffed into one doctrinal category [514F.2d at 676] " (Kaplin, 1978, p. 180).

new. It was the basis for at least one decision in the nineteenth century—*Niedermeyer* v. *Curators of the University of Missouri* (1895) (Peterson, 1970, pp. 260-266), but the court's acceptance of the catalog as a contract in academic matters is new. In the 1976 case of *Lyons* v. *Salve Regina College*, a student who was dismissed from college on the basis of failing a course was ordered readmitted by the U.S. District Court because the appeals process did not conform with the procedures outlined in the college catalog. The decision was overturned by the U.S. Court of Appeals, not on the grounds that the catalog was not a contract, but because it believed the procedures to have been in compliance with the catalog. This decision is currently being appealed to the U.S. Supreme Court. In the 1978 case of *Goldberg* v. *Chicago Medical School,* a rejected applicant won a fraud and damage suit on the grounds that a college used procedures for admitting students other than those explicitly stated in its catalog—"academic achievement, Medical College Admission test results, personal appraisals by a preprofessional advisory committee or individual instructors. . . ." The Illinois Supreme Court accepted Goldberg's contention that Chicago Medical School "made admissions decisions . . . on the basis of how much money applicants and the families could contribute to the school" ("Unsuccessful Medical School Applicant Wins Fraud Suit Against College," 1978).

Financial Aid and Tuition

Student rights and institutional responsibilities in this area include:

1. Students and potential students should be informed of the full cost of education.
2. Students and potential students should be informed about the financial aid programs available to them, exemplary financial aid packages, the procedures for obtaining aid, and the criteria for awarding aid.
3. Accurate and up-to-date information should be offered on the financial aid available.
4. Loan applicants should be informed of the source of their loans, loan repayment obligations and procedures, loan

repayment schedules and consequences of not paying, and means of cancelling or deferring payments.

5. Fair and adequate refund policies should be employed, including offering refunds, having a written refund policy, publicly disseminating that policy, informing students of how to get refunds, specifying a maximum time between receipt of a valid refund request and the actual refund, basing refunds on the amount of instruction received, and conforming to stated refund policies.

6. Fair and reasonable fees should be charged for infractions such as breaking laboratory equipment or losing a library book.

7. Tuition increases should be reasonable and adequate notice of raises should be given.

8. Student tuition payments should be safeguarded and records should be kept of the fees each student has paid.

9. Student loan defaults and other financial aid abuses should be discouraged.

10. Students should be informed about institutional financial instability, if such a condition exists.

A study by Sandra Willett (1976) revealed that a number of institutions were not carrying out their responsibilities in providing financial aid information. Willett, former director of consumer education at the Department of Health, Education, and Welfare, sent a letter as a potential student requesting information on the financial aid that might be available for her to go to college to each of the 77 postsecondary institutions in the city of Boston that participate in any of the five major Office of Education federal student aid programs. Thirty-two of her letters were directed at degree-granting colleges. Nearly one third (10) of them failed to respond. In the larger study of postsecondary schools, 32 percent failed to respond and 22 percent more failed to mention the programs in which they were eligible to participate.

As noted earlier, incomplete reporting of financial aid information was also found in 17 percent of the 1975 catalogs examined in the Carnegie Council staff catalog study. Some out-of-date information was also encountered. In addition, 30 percent of undergraduates who have had financial advising found it "not very adequate" (Carnegie Surveys, 1975-76).

The College Scholarship Service believes this gap in information is significant, citing the following examples:

A 1974 survey in New Jersey showed that only 44 percent of all college students had applied for financial aid from their institutions. More than a quarter of the students from families with incomes below $6,000 (students who can almost certainly be assumed to have financial need) failed to apply for aid. More than 4 out of 10 students from families with incomes of between $6,000 and $12,000 failed to apply for institutional aid. And three quarters of the students who were residents of New Jersey failed to apply to the state's grant program for assistance. When asked why not, over two thirds cited lack of information.

Other statewide studies show numerous low-income students failing to apply for aid. In a 1975 Pennsylvania study nearly 1 out of 5 enrolled students from families with incomes of less than $9,000 failed to apply for aid. A 1972 California study showed that nearly two thirds of the low-income respondents had not filed for aid. In Oregon that same year, more than 4 out of 10 students from families with incomes less than $6,000 failed to apply for aid. A 1971 study in the State of Washington put that number at 6 out of 10. . . .

[And sadly] a 1972 study of high school seniors found that 33 percent of those who did not continue their education gave as a reason that they could not afford it [College Entrance Examination Board, 1977, p. 11].

On refund policies, Jung and others' study (1976) of more than 5,500 students at eight degree-granting institutions reported that 16 percent were not informed of their school's policy for refunding fees and charges. This year, the Union for Experimenting Colleges filed a bankruptcy petition because it was at least a quarter of a million dollars in debt. Eighty-five thousand dollars of this debt were for overdue student tuition rebates (Middleton, 1978, p. 1). The nonrefund policies of un-accredited Riverside University in California were publicized by Congressman Jerry Pettis in 1974. Riverside, which was closed for improper practices, failed to notify students that loans had been received or to refund loans when students withdrew prior to actual enrollment (Special Subcommittee on Education, 1974).

A similarly sensational occurrence has been revealed with regard to tuition handling in the case of Harry Lowther, whose financial activities closed faltering Prescott College in Arizona and fledgling Lincoln Open University in Illinois ("Figure in Scandal Sentenced to Prison," 1978, p. 2; Van Dyne, 1978, p. 2). More common are complaints about the handling of tuition in off-campus programs run by profit-making companies, in which tuition is collected by the company rather than the college or university sponsoring the program (Watkins, 1977). We read occasionally in trade or local newspapers of a financial aid officer coaching students on loan cheating, even at regionally accredited institutions ("Former Financial Aid Officer Charged with Embezzlement," 1977, p. 2; "Texas Student-Aid Officer Indicted on Fraud Charge," 1977, p. 2). And the Veterans Administration reported mounting evidence that many veterans, "often with active encouragement and complicity of certain schools," are enrolling in courses not to pursue an education but to receive benefits (U.S. Senate, 1976, p. 47).

In summary, the tuition and financial aid situation appears to be this: Intentionally abusive institutions such as Riverside are few in number. More common has been a sloughing of responsibility by some institutions as described by Willet and Jung. However, the practices they reported are now covered by the "Student Consumer Information" provisions of the Education Amendments of 1976, which were already discussed under "Institutional Advertising." Our recommendations for dealing with other financial aid problems are in Section 4.

Some federal programs have gone beyond requiring colleges and universities to provide information. The Veterans Administration currently requires refunds no smaller than the prorated cost of the time attended minus 10 percent, a policy strongly criticized by selective institutions, and requires those refunds within 40 days of a student's withdrawal from school. Proposed U.S. Office of Education Guaranteed Student Loan regulations require "a fair and equitable refund policy" based on length of time enrolled and the nature of instruction provided as well as a 40-day refund deadline. Extension of these regulations to all Title IV programs (college work-study, Basic Educational Opportunity Grants, Supplemental Educational Opportunity Grants, and National Direct Student Loans) is also being considered ("Extention of GSL Policy Proposed in New Regulations," 1978). In addition, new Title IV regulations were recently proposed, including a requirement that institutions bond financial aid officers at 10 percent of the amount of aid distributed by the college, a requirement that institutions present a certified financial statement on request by the U.S. Commissioner of Education, and a list of "warning signals" for institutional financial instability that will be used to limit, suspend, or terminate a college's participation in these programs ("OE Proposes to Clean Up Student Aid Programs," 1978).

At the state level, requirements are less stiff—only 8 states have statutes or regulations governing minimum refund policies and practices in private degree-granting colleges; 11 have statutes and regulations concerning financial practices of private degree-granting institutions such as procedures for loan awards, requirements for fees, or requirements for scholarship or aid; and 19 have statutes and laws on the financial stability of private degree granters. In the public sector, 8 states have statutes and regulations on the subject of refund (for example, Connecticut and Virginia require that a "fair and equitable refund policy" be established and described in a school's catalog) and 28 states have statutes and regulations dealing with financial practices (Jung and others, 1977).

The courts have not been a significant factor in this area, though they have ruled in favor of nonresident tuition. However, a very interesting case is currently in the making. Eighty percent of the sophomore and junior classes at Northwestern University Medical School are suing their college over a 57 percent increase in tuition. They charge that the raise constitutes an abrupt increase beyond the fees listed in the university catalog.

The Council on Postsecondary Accreditation reports that the regional associations have long been interested in tuition and financial aid abuses, but concern with responsibility is increasing. Several of the member associations have, for example, produced guidelines on refund policy.

As for institutions, one of the consequences of the Fund for the Improvement of Postsecondary Education's "Better Information for Student Choice" project has been the creation of model tuition and financial aid statements. For example, the Barat College prospectus contains information on the total costs of education, foregone earnings, the likelihood of tuition increases, comparative tuition costs, thorough answers to 19 of the most common questions about financial aid, and sample financial aid packages for students from three diverse families.

Student organizations have also been active in this area, especially the National Student Educational Fund (NSEF) and the National Student Lobby (NSL) (which recently merged with the National Student Association to form the U.S. Student Association). NSEF is responsible for the production of a three-volume report entitled *The Options Handbook* (1976). Volume two is concerned strictly with costs and financial aid. NSL has actively engaged in lobbying on financial aid issues and is given a share of the credit for the passage of the peer counseling provision of the Education Amendments of 1976 which requires the U.S. Office of Education to study the use of students as financial aid counselors and, wherever possible, to include them in training sessions.

Important nonsocial policy developments off-campus include another product of the National Task Force on Better Information for Student Choice, entitled *Making It Count: A Report on a Project to Provide Better Financial Aid Information to Students* (1978), and the rise of brokerage organizations, designed to provide people who are not attending institutions of higher education with low- or no-cost outreach advising on educational services and their cost. As of 1978 the National Center for Educational Brokerage listed 200 such organizations around the country (Levine, 1978, p. 152).

Admissions

In this area, student rights and institutional responsibilities include the following:

1. Written policies on recruiting and admissions should be available.
2. Students should be admitted on the basis of a publicly announced admissions policy.
3. A professional admissions staff should be employed and salaries should not be based primarily on the number of students enrolled.
4. Prospective students should be given as complete and accurate a picture of an institution as possible. They should be encouraged to visit the campus and speak with faculty and students when possible.
5. Institutional services or benefits such as job placement or particular vocational programs should be clearly and specifically described.
6. Compensatory or support services should be available for students lacking the ability to complete institutional requirements at the time of admission.
7. Orientation should be offered to all newly enrolled students.

Many colleges are in serious need of students, and the students they are able to recruit are different from those of previous years—they are less able in basic skills, and a higher proportion of them are nontraditional students. In general, institutions are facing growing competition to attract such students and increasing diversity in what they must offer to meet such students' needs. This burden has caused some colleges to compromise their admissions responsibilities.

Based on self-reports of college officials, Jung and others (1976) found several instances of institutional laxness in a study of 12 accredited degree-granting institutions. Of the sample:

• Five institutions had no written policy governing recruiting and/or admissions.
• One institution stated in its advertising that the education or training it offered was likely to lead to employment.
• One institution employed admissions representatives whose compensation was based wholly or in part on commissions.
• Five institutions admitted students who did not meet stated admissions requirements and offered no remedial courses in basic mathematics.
• Three institutions admitted students who did not meet stated admissions requirements and offered no remedial courses in basic English.

Daniel Muñoz (Muñoz and Garcia-Bahne, 1978), a psychologist at the University of California, San Diego, believes that particular groups of students are being admitted to college without needed support services. He points to a pattern of academic problems, low support services, probation, and dropout among Chicano students whose graduation rate from college (24 percent) is half of that of whites (48 percent). In a study of selected Chicano students at two University of California campuses and two California State University campuses, Muñoz found that 72 percent of the Chicano dropouts in the sample had been on academic probation and only 33 percent of the enrolled Chicanos received tutorial or other academic support services.

In addition, a College Board panel on international education found that American universities were eagerly pursuing foreign students, often without adequate review of their qualifications. The chairman of the panel, Clifford F. Sjogren, Jr., charged " 'hucksterism' by some institutions and a fairly widespread tendency to admit foreign students who are unqualified" because of declining domestic enrollments ("Colleges Warned of Danger in Admitting Foreign Students Who Lack Qualifications," 1977, p. 6). Indeed, as was mentioned in Section 1, foreign student enrollments rose by 13 percent from 179,340 to 203,070 in a single academic year, 1976-77 to 1977-78. At two-year colleges, the proportion of foreign students increased from 10.6 percent of total enrollments in 1970 to 15.6 percent in 1976. The largest increases have been from wealthy underdeveloped nations. For instance, 25.6 percent of foreign students now come from the OPEC nations ("203,068 Foreign Students Enroll at U.S. Colleges: 23,310 from Iran," 1978, p. 13).

One also occasionally hears stories about students admitted to college for the wrong reasons. When the *Bakke* case broke, reports were published regarding the practice at the University of California, Davis, of reserving several places in its medical school class for "friends" of the university. In the *Goldberg* v. *Chicago Medical School* case, noted earlier, the plaintiff won a fraud suit because the university admitted students, at least in part, on the basis of their ability to support the school, rather than the criteria listed in the catalog. According to another source, "In a few states—Illinois, New York, and Pennsylvania—indications are that the practice of admitting students for nonacademic reasons may be more widespread than officials would like to admit. In Pennsylvania, for example, court records indicate that parents and friends have paid hundreds of thousands of dollars to assure the acceptance of dozens of students" ("Charges of Admission Peddling Prompt Federal and State Probes," 1978, p. 3).

Pressure to increase enrollments sometimes unintentionally results in flagging responsibility. For example, within five minutes an admissions officer at an accredited and straight-laced private, midwestern religious college engaged in both "bait and switch"—attracting a student by offering one program and substituting another—and "negative sell"—making an institution attractive on the basis of exclusive or selective characteristics which it does not in fact possess. He told a prospective student about a new vocational program the school had created and informed the student who had a low grade-point average from high school that he would probably be able to gain admission to the college. The fact of the matter is that the appealing vocational program was not yet fully operational and would almost certainly be filled by upperclassmen once it was in operation, so that the student would probably find just a traditional liberal arts program after he enrolled. This is "bait and switch." In addition, the applicant would, without a doubt, be admitted since the college was virtually open admission but did not announce it. That is "negative sell." Some other colleges engage in similar practices—listing vocational programs prominently in the catalogs or promotional literature without explaining they are oversubscribed with waiting lists. If students are drawn to college on the basis of such recruiting and do not get the programs they expect that is also "bait and switch."

One California community college engages in a different type of inappropriate practice. In at least one vocational program, it admits students from a long waiting list throughout the term to replace dropouts. Prospective replacement students, who will lose at least a portion of the term but save the college money by filling otherwise vacant classroom seats, are contacted and guaranteed admission when an opening occurs, but if the offer is declined they are told, in truth, that they may not be admitted at the start of a new term for some time to come owing to the long waiting list.

In summary, some colleges, including a number of respected institutions, have been less than fully responsible in the way they handle admissions. However, as with each of the three issue areas examined previously, the evidence does not indicate that irresponsibility is flagrant.

Admissions policy, like academic programming, has traditionally been thought of as the province of colleges and universities, and, like academic programming, this is changing. Of the social policy agencies that have become involved, the courts have been the most active and encroached deepest into institutional prerogatives. In the cases of *DeFunis* v. *Odegaard* and *Bakke* v. *The Regents of the University of California*, the courts have ruled on the appropriate criteria for college admissions. In the case of *Goldberg* v. *Chicago Medical School*, the courts ruled on the discretion of colleges to depart from their published admissions criteria. In the case of *Barnes* v. *Converse College*, the court ruled on the extent of support services that students must be offered to compensate for deficiencies existing at the time of admission. Converse College was ordered to provide an interpreter for a deaf student. This decision was recently overturned, but appeals continue. However, the courts' initial finding was upheld in the August 1978 case of two deaf students who obtained a U.S. district court preliminary injunction requiring the California State University, Hayward, to provide them with interpreters (*Daily Californian*, 1978, p. 17).

The executive and legislative branches of the federal government have also become increasingly involved in admissions policy, although not in any particularly organized fashion. A variety of laws and agencies touch upon admissions policy in a number of different ways. For example, Title VI of the 1964 Civil Rights Act, as extended through the Education Act Amendments, prohibits discrimination in college admissions on the basis of a student's sex, race, color, or place of national origin. The Veterans Administration, through Public Law 92-540, determines the time that enrollment to college becomes final for recipients of veterans benefits. A ten-day cooling off period is provided to deter high-pressure sales and on-the-spot enrollment agreements. The Guaranteed Student Loan program requires institutions to show that the students they admit have the ability to benefit from the instruction or training they offer; also required are data on withdrawal rates, failure rates, placement rates, grades, or other performance criteria. Recently proposed regulations for the five major Office of Education financial aid programs require that colleges maintain student admissions records for the purpose of determining whether they meet the legal definition of a higher education institution ("Rules Proposed for Participation in Aid Programs," 1978, p. 5).

State statutes and regulations are much the same as in the other three issue areas. Nineteen states have rather general statutes and regulations on admissions policy in private degree-granting institutions and six have statutes and regulations on recruiting agents in private degree-granting institutions. (Only Kentucky holds institutions responsible for their recruiters' actions and the other five states, in varying degree, prohibit false, deceptive, misleading, or unfair practices by agents.) In the public sector, more than half of the states have some statutes or regulations relating to admission, but only a very few specify policies (Jung and others, 1977).

Admissions policy is an area of concern to accrediting associations, but their record here is mixed. Several regional associations, including the North Central Association, have been pushing colleges to be more vigilant about the ability of the students they admit, but on the issue of admitting ill-prepared foreign students there has been some hemming and hawing.

At the institutional level, some schools are providing better support services for ill-prepared enrollees. Exemplary of such efforts is the HELP (Higher Education for Low-Income People) Center at the University of Minnesota. Funded by private, local, state, and federal money, it provides students with welfare and housing advice, employment and financial counseling, and academic tutoring. Approximately 1,000 University of Minnesota students utilize HELP services and those who do have lower attrition rates and higher grade-point averages than similar students who do not.

Other institutions, such as the University of California, San Diego, are trying to reach students and parents before higher education to notify them about the skills needed for college level study. At San Diego, a flyer has been prepared to warn parents about the negative consequences for their children if they do not take mathematics in high school.

A number of schools are getting faculty and students more involved with admissions, either by sending them out to recruit alone or with an admissions officer, as at Brandeis University, or in reviewing admissions publications, as at the University of California, Irvine.

4

Recommendations

As a consequence of the state of affairs described in the preceding sections, the Carnegie Council offers the following agenda for action.

Students

If students are to protect their rights and take advantage of their opportunities, they must be better educated in consumer skills.

Recommendation 1. *Local schools and school districts should make consumer education available to students and their parents early enough to influence student curricular and life choices.*

- Information on postsecondary education and financial aid opportunities should be sent to parents, and informational sessions should be held for them before their children enter senior high school and make the critical decisions about foreign language and mathematics that will significantly affect college and career access.
- Formal discussion of education and life planning should begin for students in junior high school.
- A course on postsecondary opportunities should be offered in the high schools prior to the senior year. The course should explore postsecondary alternatives—the options, education as well as work, that exist for students leaving high school, how

to find out more about these options, and how to decide which of the options or combination of options is preferred. The course should also be concerned with financing a post-secondary education—how to estimate costs, sources of financial support, rights and responsibilities of the aid recipient, sources of financial aid information, and how and when to apply for aid. Such a course has been designed by Kevin Bacon and the National Student Educational Fund.

- Schools should purchase and encourage students to use low-cost materials such as *Safeguarding Your Education: A Student Consumer Guide to College and Occupational Education.* This particular product, which consists of two casette tapes and a "Student's Consumer Guidebook," has the twin virtues of being engaging to young people and quite valuable in teaching basic educational consumer skills.

Recommendation 2. *Broad-based Educational Information Centers, created by the Education Amendments of 1976 and currently being initiated on a small scale, should be fully funded to provide a complete range of information on educational alternatives, requirements, rights and responsibilities, and financial aid options; comparative data on institutions; guidance and counseling; and referral services to all people and schools desiring to use these services in every state.*

- A major function of the centers should be consumer education outreach, particularly for adults and others who will not have benefit of the proposed high school course. The states and their schools should use the services of centers in preparing consumer education programs for parents and students.
- A second major function should be to make education and career information readily available in convenient locations such as schools, shopping centers, work places, and community centers. A useful model is the Oregon Career Information System, which is an easily operated, computerized data bank relying upon simple English commands and containing information on job descriptions, necessary job skills, required training, places offering training, requirements for admission to training, and manpower projections.

• The Educational Information Centers in each state should issue periodic reports on noteworthy new information to the schools and student newspapers.

Recommendation 3. *The Fund for the Improvement of Post-secondary Education and other foundations with educational missions should support and evaluate alternative models of consumer education.*

In addition to the measures that we recommend that schools, colleges, and other agencies adopt to improve student information, we believe students, as consumers, should take more of the initiative in becoming informed. To assist them, we offer the following checklist:

Questions Students Should Ask About a College (After Deciding to Continue Their Education Beyond High School)

BEFORE ENROLLING
1. What are the entrance requirements?
2. What are the requirements for completing a course, program, or degree?
3. Who are the faculty?
4. What support services does this institution offer (for example, counseling, health care, compensatory education, job placement)?
5. What kind of learning environment is offered (for example, teaching methods, scope of programs, class size, transferability of credits, library, postgraduate activities of alumni)?
6. Are the types of equipment and facilities I need for my education available?
7. What are the total student costs of attendance, the types of financial aid available, the terms for receiving aid, the amount of financial aid that can be counted on, and the circumstances and extent to which tuition and fee refunds are available?
8. Is there a code of ethics, disciplinary policy, and grievance procedures that I can agree to comply with?

9. Are there minimum standards of acceptable performance below which a student may be put on probation or expelled?
10. Is this institution equipped to serve my personal and academic needs?

AFTER ENROLLING

11. When and what types of orientation are available?
12. Are instruction, programs, staff, support services, facilities, grievance procedures, and institutional learning environment of the quality and quantity promised? Do they meet my needs?
13. Are faculty available outside of class?
14. Are evaluation and the award of credit meaningful, timely, and based wholly on academic criteria?
15. Are program changes made which set back or impede my academic program?
16. Are tuition increases reasonable and announced in timely fashion?
17. Am I conscientiously planning, monitoring, and carrying out my education?
18. Am I fulfilling my ethical responsibilities in a manner consistent with the institutional code of rights and responsibilities?
19. If attending a branch or off-campus center, is the program equivalent in quality to that of the institution's home campus?

Institutions

The Carnegie Council believes that, to fulfill its mission, higher education must be an ethical community. Emphasis should be placed on defining the rights and responsibilities of students and their colleges. Those listed in Sections 2 and 3 provide a general model and convenient checklist by which students and colleges can evaluate their conduct. However, specific statements of rights and responsibilities must be geared to the character of an individual campus and the students who attend it.

Recommendation 4. *Every institution of higher education that has not already done so should produce a code of rights and responsibilities through the collaborative efforts of administrators, faculty, and students.* Codes intended to guide the student-college relationship should address the subjects of admissions, recruiting, advertising, financial aid, tuition, record keeping, instruction, academic requirements, advising, grievance procedures, support services, and student conduct. With the exception of grievance procedures and student conduct, all of these topics are covered in the lists of rights and responsibilities found in Sections 2 and 3. Grievance procedures will be discussed in item 6 below.

A sizeable proportion of institutions already have codes for students, faculty, administrators, or some combination thereof. For instance, 69 percent of the colleges and universities questioned in the 1978 Carnegie Council survey had a code for their faculty.[1] The proportion varies by institutional types as shown in Table 5. However, many of the codes have proven ineffective. This appears to occur most frequently when a code does not represent a consensus of faculty, administrative, and student opinion; when a code is vague; when it does not cover important areas of activity; when violations of a code are winked at or ignored; and when a code is no longer relevant to a campus's situation.

National higher education associations with institutional membership can assist in the process. In this regard, the Council applauds the achievements of the American Council on Education (ACE) for its creation of a model code of institutional fair practice, the establishment of a new office concerned with higher education self-regulation, and a variety of other related activities too numerous to list here.

---

[1]The survey asked about faculty codes in general, rather than a specific type of code, which accounts in part for the high positive response rate. It should also be noted that having a faculty code does not mean an institution also has a student, administrative, or institutional code.

Table 5. Percentages of colleges and universities with Faculty
Codes of Academic Conduct, by Carnegie type

Research universities I	66
Research universities II	78
Doctorate-granting universities I	58
Doctorate-granting universities II	81
Comprehensive universities and colleges I	74
Comprehensive universities and colleges II	65
Liberal arts colleges I	61
Liberal arts colleges II	74
Two-year colleges and institutes	67
Average	69

Source: Carnegie Surveys, 1978.

Recommendation 5. *Colleges and universities should publish statements of the range of penalties that will be imposed for general classes of violations of their rights and firmly administer the penalties for infractions.* Institutions must not reward academic dishonesty. Penalties for willful dishonesty must be severe because truth is the stock and trade of the academic community.

Another requirement for protecting student and institutional rights is an understandable system of handling grievances.

Recommendation 6. *Institutions should develop equitable, easily navigable, and publicized grievance procedures.* Colleges and universities should consider appointing an institutionwide ombudsperson. At small colleges, where the ombudsperson would have little business, the job might be a part-time position. In any event, it should be filled by an individual acceptable to faculty, students, and administrators.

With regard to a grievance system, Joan Stark (1977, pp. 193-194)[2] has recommended that it include the following elements:

[2]Reprinted by permission of the publisher, from Joan S. Stark, *The Many Faces of Educational Consumerism* (Lexington, Massachusetts: Lexington Books, D. C. Heath and Company, copyright 1977, D. C. Heath and Company).

- Informal resolution of a problem should precede use of formal mechanisms.
- Resolution should take place at the lowest level in the organization. If necessary, a mutually agreed-upon third party should mediate informally; a third party mediator should be appointed if the parties are unable to select one.
- Formal grievance procedures should begin only when [the above] have been unsuccessful and the grievant petitions for a hearing.
- The system should provide a speedy resolution of conflict.
- The grievance system should be sufficiently flexible to deal with simple cases and also with complex ones.
- The grievance process should be encumbered as little as possible with the trappings of legal terminology and court mechanics. The spirit of impartiality is more important than its outward symbols.
- Local considerations should be taken into account; grievance procedures should reflect the character of the institution. It is not possible to specify a procedure that will work on every campus.
- Large institutions should decentralize grievance boards to at least the college level.
- Large institutions should have hearing boards which deal with different substantive matters in which members develop some expertise and experience. Provision must be made for assigning cases to the proper board.
- Small institutions might increase fairness by developing a hearing board in consort with other nearby colleges and choosing members at random from among the institutions.
- The system should provide for impartial selection of hearing board members from various peer groups.
- Unless there is some compelling reason why grievances which have reached the formal hearing stage should be closed, public proceedings will assure the community that the system is working and increase the value of fair practice.[3]
- The system should provide for an adequate transcript of pro-

[3]The Council believes closed proceedings may be more desirable in a variety of circumstances, particularly if the grievant requests that the proceedings not be public.

ceedings; precedents from previous decisions should be available for review by disputants.[4]

- The fact that a student brings a grievance should not be noted on his permanent record unless he wishes to make disagreement with a final decision a matter of record.
- Grievance procedures and the philosophy on which they are based should be made available in published form to all members of the campus community, along with information which assists in gaining ready access to the system.

The Carnegie Council endorses these principles with a warning. These formal procedures assume good will on the part of the participants. Formal grievance procedures should not be used as a political forum for deciding controversial issues such as stock disinvestment policy, nor should they be used to adjudicate petty or insignificant problems. Formal grievance procedures can be expensive for an institution if overused, and the cost can be treated as a weapon to harrass an institution or blackmail it into concessions.

Recommendation 7. *Institutions should voluntarily embrace the principle of full and complete disclosure, and provide students with comprehensive and accurate information on all pertinent aspects of institutional practice, including basic institutional identification and rules of governance; financial costs and student financial obligations; educational resources, process, and content; and indications of institutional effectiveness.* Institutions of higher education should gradually move toward catalogs such as that of Barat College. Institutions will benefit as much from such a policy as students will. First, better information should lead to better decision making by students and hence reduce attrition. Second, since several recent court decisions have held the college catalog to constitute a contract between the student and his or her school, a more accurate document will reduce the likelihood of lawsuits. Third, full and

---

[4]The Council favors a summary transcript rather than a verbatim transcript which is a very expensive and generally not particularly useful document.

complete disclosure can be a vehicle for turning a college's desired purposes and goals into a self-fulfilling prophecy by attracting faculty and students committed to those programs and goals. Fourth and finally, if institutions do not choose to move toward full and complete disclosure of their own volition, it is quite likely, on the basis of additional court decisions and legislation, such as the "Student Consumer Information Services" provision of the Education Amendments of 1976, that they will be compelled to do so anyway, but with less flexibility than voluntary action would permit now.

College and university trustees should regularly review the state of institutional responsibility by asking the following questions about both on- and off-campus programs:

Trustee's Checklist of Basic Institutional Responsibilities

1. Does this institution have a realistic, equitable, and up-to-date code of rights and responsibilities?
2. Is institutional advertising and admissions literature, such as the college catalog, complete, accurate, up to date, understandable, and intended to serve as a contract between the institution and its students?
3. Are students given complete, accurate, and up-to-date information about the full cost of education, the financial aids available, and the financial status of the institution?
4. Are chartered, approved, and accredited status accurately and completely described in institutional literature?
5. Are recruiting and admissions staff members professionals who admit only those students who are capable of benefiting from the institution's academic programs?
6. Are students provided with an orientation when they first enroll?
7. Are refund policies for tuition and other fees fair, accurate, and publicly disseminated?
8. Are institutional requirements educationally meaningful; described in clear, specific, and accurate form; and subject to change only with advance notice in a manner that will not impede the progress of students who are already enrolled?

9. Are instructional programs, facilities, and equipment adequate, up to date, and accurately described in institutional publications?
10. Are evaluation (grading) and the award of credit fair, meaningful, timely, and based wholly on academic criteria?
11. Are student cheating and other forms of academic dishonesty actively discouraged by the institution?
12. Do faculty have a relatively low turnover rate and appropriate training?
13. Are students provided with services of the quality and quantity they have been promised, particularly with regard to job placement, compensatory education, courses of study, and counseling?
14. Are tuition increases reasonable and are students given adequate notice of them?
15. Does the institution periodically conduct a self-study of the state of rights and responsibilities on campus and issue annual reports in problem areas describing the ameliorative steps which have been taken and the results of these efforts?

Accreditation

Accrediting associations are involved in issues of rights and responsibilities in two ways—through their traditional roles as voluntary, private membership organizations whose primary function it is to pass on whether institutions or programs have attained their stated purposes and to make recommendations for improvement; and, more recently, through federal and state requirements that institutions be accredited by recognized associations as a condition for participation in certain programs, particularly U.S. Office of Education student aid.

The Carnegie Council believes that accreditation should build upon state licensure which defines a minimum permissable level of institutional activity. Accreditation should start at that floor and seek to improve the standing of an institution. It should, as a result, imply a higher level of quality and more select standing than state licensing. The emphasis in this report is on regional accreditation which is concerned with the whole of an institution and its educational activities in their entirety.

Recommendation 8. *Regional accrediting associations should serve as the primary external actor in matters of institutional rights and responsibilities for accredited colleges.*

The federal government has chosen to use accreditation as one of the principal criteria for judging institutional eligibility to participate in more than 60 programs administered by at least 8 federal agencies, and the Council urges that practice to be continued. At the same time, the Council is aware that there have been criticisms of accrediting associations for lax standards and unreliable performance within a number of states, such as Texas, and some elements of the federal government, such as the Veterans Administration. Accrediting associations are a diverse group. Some are doing very adequate jobs, a number are not. In general, improvement is necessary.

Recommendation 9. *Regional associations should (1) increase the thoroughness of institutional visits; (2) place greater emphasis upon reviewing ethical conduct in general, as defined by the responsibilities listed in Sections 2 and 3, and in particular by reviewing institutional advertising, policies for awarding credit, and catalogs as full disclosure statements intended to serve as a contract between the student and the college; (3) seek out eminently qualified people from around the country to serve on visiting teams; (4) consult with other professional associations and societies in developing academic program evaluation criteria and in identifying qualified people for visiting committees; (5) increase the number of trained full-time staff to assist visiting teams; (6) publish periodically a report on the status of all schools that are members or have applied for membership; and (7) embrace the principle of full disclosure by publishing the final institutional evaluation reports produced following accrediting team visits and publicly expose institutions engaging in bad practice.* These changes will entail additional costs to regional associations, but member institutions should be willing to assume them. They are likely to be repaid with interest in terms of future public regulations avoided and the identification of inadequate institutions and programs that would otherwise embarrass the higher education community.

The Carnegie Council is pleased that rights and responsibilities appear to be occupying an increasingly important role in the accrediting agenda. The Council also salutes the three regional associations that pioneered in the use of the Institutional Self-Study Form (ISSF), a self-administered checklist on institutional irresponsibility developed by the American Institutes for Research as part of the institutional self-study process (Dayton and Jung, 1978).

Recommendation 10. *All of the regional associations should make certain that the off-campus programs of their member institutions meet minimum standards appropriate to higher education and are comparable in quality to the standards expected of on-campus programs.* Off-campus programs should be evaluated regardless of where in the country they are located. The future of accrediting depends on it. Important first steps have been taken in this regard by the Council on Postsecondary Accreditation, which has completed a Project to Develop Evaluative Criteria and Procedures for the Accreditation of Nontraditional Education and launched an evaluation of off-campus programs offered on a number of military bases.

As a check on responsibility, accrediting associations should address the following questions about institutions and themselves:

Basic Questions Accrediting Associations Should Ask

ABOUT COLLEGES AND UNIVERSITIES

1. Is the institution financially stable?
2. Is institutional advertising accurate and complete?
3. Are institutional recruiting practices fair?
4. Is institutional disclosure of necessary information to students and prospective students adequate?
5. Is the institutional catalog treated as a full and complete disclosure statement intended to serve as a contract between the students and the college?
6. Are institutional instructional programs and facilities ade-

quate and appropriate in quality for an institution of higher education?

7. Are the institution's off-campus programs equal in quality to its on-campus programs?
8. Are institutional faculty and staff competent and appropriate in quality for an institution of higher education?
9. Are institutional record keeping policies and practices adequate?
10. Are institutional tuition and fee refund policies fair and equitable?
11. Does this institution have a code of rights and responsibilities?
12. Does this institution discourage grade inflation, academic dishonesty, financial aid abuse, poor support services, and students' failure to take responsibility for their educations?
13. Does this institution accurately represent accredited or approved status?

ABOUT THEMSELVES

14. Are institutional visits sufficiently frequent and thorough to permit comprehensive and up-to-date institutional evaluation?
15. Are visiting teams composed of the best qualified people in the country?
16. Does the association employ a sufficient number of trained, full-time staff members to assist each institutional visiting team?
17. Does this association publish a report annually on the status of all schools that are members or have applied for membership?
18. Does this association publish the final institutional evaluation reports produced following accrediting team visits and publicize institutions engaging in bad practice?
19. Does this association have a fast, equitable, comprehensive, and well-publicized grievance mechanism for handling complaints by or about member institutions?
20. Is ethical conduct (the state of rights and responsibilities on

campus) a priority item on this association's agenda and a required part of the institutional self-study procedure?

The States

The Council recognizes that state agencies have an important role to play in the student-institutional relationship, beyond the roles of the institutions themselves and of the accrediting agencies. Education is a state responsibility. Every school in the nation, with the few exceptions that include the military academies, exists by permission of a state. Chartering, setting minimum standards for the incorporation of a nonprofit organization, licensing, setting minimum standards for the award of degrees or for institutions entitled to call themselves colleges are the vehicles that states use for authorizing educational institutions. Incorporation is a requirement in every state, licensure is not. As shown in Sections 2 and 3, the comprehensiveness of existing state authorization statutes and regulations varies widely. As a consequence, some states have been more hospitable than others to irresponsible institutional and student practices that have provided the primary rationale for federal intervention.

To eliminate the now-overlapping federal-state role, it is necessary for the states to fulfill their constitutionally assigned role and assume primary responsibility for education within their boundaries. Each state must set minimum standards for approving educational institutions.

Recommendation 11. *Each state that has not already done so should adopt standards comparable to those proposed in the Education Commission of the States' Model State Legislation for approval of postsecondary educational institutions and the authorization to grant degrees.* This document covers course length, content, goals, and objectives; degrees, diplomas, credentials, and graduation requirements; qualifications of instructional and administrative staff; facilities; financial stability; public disclosure of material facts; advertising and sales recruiting practices; record keeping; financial practices; and refund policies. Jung and others (1977a) have compared how state licensing laws and regulations as of January 1977 contrast with the provisions of the model legislation. With two exceptions, most states have no laws in any of these areas for private degree-granting institutions. This is shown in Table 6.

Table 6. Summary of coverage ratings of state licensing laws and regulations in comparison with ECS model state legislation[a]

	Private degree-granting institutions				
	++	+	=	−	0
A. Institutional purpose, governance, and operation	7	13	1	0	30
B. Course length, content, goals or objectives	3	12	10	1	25
C. Degree, diploma, credential, or graduation requirements	3	13	6	1	28
D. Qualifications of instructional or administrative staff (including maximum teaching loads and teacher-pupil ratios)	5	15	5	2	24
E. Facilities (including instructional and administrative facilities and equipment, housing or room/board facilities, health and safety requirements)	1	16	7	3	24
F. Financial stability (including institutional performance bonds and financial record maintenance)	2	7	7	13	22
G. Minimum qualifications of potential students and orientation of entering students	0	18	2	0	31
H. Public disclosure of material facts (including fees and content of enrollment agreement or contracts)	2	7	3	8	31
I. Advertising or sales/recruiting practices (including minimum qualifications for licensing of sales representatives, and limitations on use of terminology such as "university," "approval," "admissions counselor," etc.)	2	1	4	17	27
J1. Student and personnel recordkeeping practices (including minimum requirements for content of students' records)	0	7	6	6	32

(continued on next page)

Table 6 *(continued)*

	Private degree-granting institutions				
	++	+	=	−	0
J2. Student and personnel recordkeeping practices (including minimum requirements for maintenance of students' records)	0	1	6	12	32
K. Financial practices (including procedures for making loan awards, requirements for fees, and scholarships or aid requirements)	0	2	9	1	39
L. Minimum refund policies and practices	0	3	4	2	42
M. Placement (including follow-up data collection from former students, graduates, employers regarding posteducation outcomes)	0	7	0	0	44
N. Other topics of possible importance for student consumer protection	1	17	0	0	27
Totals	26	139	76	66	458

++ State has much more extensive coverage than ECS
+   State has more extensive coverage than ECS
=   State has equally extensive coverage as ECS
−   State has less extensive coverage than ECS
0   State has no coverage or no law

^aState laws and regulations in effect as of January 1, 1977.

Source: Jung and others, 1977a.

The Council is concerned about the continued existence of degree mills.

Recommendation 12. *The states should accept the obligation for screening clearly inadequate programs offered by unaccredited colleges as part of their licensure and oversight responsibilities.* To date the state record is unsatisfactory, though by no means uniformly so. Many of the states have not fulfilled their responsibilities. For example, to establish a college in the state of California, all that is required is proof of $50,000 in assets and a statement of educational goals.

The Federal Government

The federal government's role in education is tied to the spending and commerce powers granted by the U.S. Constitution. The federal government would have minimal influence on the relationship between students and colleges if institutions chose not to participate in federally funded aid programs. This indirect influence is reflected in the checkerboard pattern of policies and regulations described in Sections 2 and 3, which are associated with different governmental programs and administered by at least 15 agencies, including the Bureau of Indian Affairs; Civil Service Commission; Department of Health, Education, and Welfare; Department of Housing and Urban Development; Federal Trade Commission; General Services Administration; Immigration and Naturalization Service; National Science Foundation; Postal Service; Veterans Administration; and Federal Interagency Committee on Education Subcommittee on Educational Consumer Protection. This state of decentralization has resulted in poor communication among participating agencies, inadequate sharing of information about irresponsible institutions and irresponsible students, such as loan defaulters, a jumble of new regulations and reporting procedures, unequal demands upon institutions and students, and slow and inadequate enforcement of existing regulations.

Recommendation 13. *The federal government should (1) place more reliance upon state government, where regulation can be geared to the needs of the individual state and enforcement can be swifter, in matters of student and institutional rights, and should reserve for itself only those areas that touch directly upon its spending powers that are out of the purview of the states (such as collection of defaulted student loans); (2) make procedural compliance with existing laws and regulations easier for institutions and students by reducing, where possible, needless diversity in policies; (3) halt further "consumer" legislation until such time as the flood of new and existing regulations can be evaluated; and (4) eliminate procedural regulations which* *substantively infringe upon academic programming, such as the Veterans Administration 12-hour rule.*

The U.S. Office of Education's Division of Eligibility and Agency Evaluation, in particular, should subject petitions for recognition by accrediting associations to stricter scrutiny by establishing minimum submission requirements, visiting a larger sample of member institutions, reviewing visiting team reports more thoroughly, actively soliciting outside opinions on associations and their member schools, and appointing to its advisory committee the best qualified people in the country. To carry out the additional field work responsibilities proposed, the division's professional staff will have to be increased. To insure that the job can be done adequately, perhaps ten more professionals will be necessary.

With regard to student loan defaults and other forms of financial aid abuse, the Carnegie Council urges that the onus of anti-abuse regulations be removed from institutions and placed squarely on the shoulders of abusive students, except as institutions encourage such abuse. The federal government should be more aggressive in trying to collect repayments and in bringing delinquent cases to court. The recent improvement in the Guaranteed Student Loan situation is an indication of what such action can accomplish.

Recommendation 14. *The passage of legislation that would allow the Internal Revenue Service to turn over to the Veterans Administration and the Department of Health, Education, and Welfare the current addresses of loan defaulters, and state legislation that would allow the garnishment of the salaries of defaulters working for the state should be considered where it has not yet been adopted.*

Except in the specific cases noted above, the Council sees no need for additional federal or state legislation at this time. However, in another report the Council does recommend substantive changes in the federal student aid system.

Who Should Do What?

The improvement of the state of rights and responsibilities in higher education rests with colleges and universities, students, and a variety of external organizations. To recapitulate, the Carnegie Council recommends that each of these groups undertake the following tasks:

Colleges and Universities

- Develop on each campus a code of rights and responsibilities for community members, through the collaborative efforts of administrators, faculty, and students
- Publish statements of the range of penalties that will be imposed for general classes of violations of institutional rights and firmly administer the penalties for infractions
- Adopt inflation-proof grading systems similar to the one proposed at the University of California, Berkeley, which would list the average grade awarded in a course in addition to the student's own in classes larger than ten
- Develop equitable, easily navigable, and widely publicized governance and grievance procedures
- Consider appointing an ombudsperson
- Voluntarily embrace the principle of full and complete disclosure, and provide students with complete and accurate information on all pertinent aspects of institutional practice, including basic institutional identification and rules of governance; financial costs and student financial obligations; educational resources, process, and content; and indications of institutional effectiveness
- Seek to resolve differences with students on campus and call upon external agencies only when on-campus remedies have been exhausted
- Voluntarily work to eliminate institutional irresponsibility
- Conduct a self-study on the state of rights and responsibilities on each campus with particular reference to the following problems—grade inflation, inferior off-campus programs, financial aid abuse, cheating, admission of unqualified students, inaccurate advertising, liberal award of credit, misuse of library resources, and inadequate support services
- If problems are discovered, in a self-study of rights and responsibilities, issue annual reports describing the steps that have been taken to solve them and the results of these efforts

Students

- Take responsibility for being informed, using available institutional resources when needed, and taking an active part in planning and formulating their education
- Seek to resolve differences with institutions on campus and call upon external agencies only when on-campus remedies have been exhausted
- Voluntarily work to eliminate student irresponsibility

Regional Accrediting Associations

- Serve as the primary external actor in matters of institutional rights and responsibilities for accredited colleges
- Increase the thoroughness of institutional visits
- Develop and enforce general codes of ethical academic conduct based on the responsibilities listed in Sections 2 and 3
- Place greater emphasis on reviewing institutional advertising, policies for awarding credit, and catalogs as full disclosure statements intended to serve as a contract between students and colleges
- Seek out eminently qualified people from around the country to serve on visiting teams
- Consult with other professional associations and societies in developing academic program evaluation criteria and in identifying the most able people for visiting committees
- Increase the number of full-time trained staff to assist such committees
- Publish periodically a report on the status of all schools that are members or have applied for membership
- Publish the final institutional evaluation reports produced following accrediting team visits and publicly expose institutions engaging in bad practice
- Apply the same academic standards for evaluating the on-campus and off-campus activities of colleges and universities
- Accept responsibility for evaluating the programs offered by all member institutions regardless of where in the country they are located

The States

- Fulfill their Constitutionally assigned role and assume primary responsibility for education within their boundaries
- Set minimum standards of institutional responsibility comparable to those proposed in the Education Commission of the States' *Model State Legislation* for the approval of postsecondary educational institutions and the authorization to grant degrees
- Pass laws allowing the garnishment of the salaries of loan defaulters working for the state
- Accept the obligation for screening clearly inferior programs offered by unaccredited colleges as part of licensure and oversight responsibilities

The Schools

- Make consumer education available to students and their parents early enough to influence student curricular and life choices
- Offer informational sessions and send literature to parents, before their children enter senior high school, about postsecondary education and financial aid opportunities
- Provide formal education and life planning sessions for students, beginning in junior high school
- Offer a course on postsecondary education to high school students prior to their senior year
- Use the services of educational information centers in preparing consumer education programs for parents and students

The Federal Government

- Place more reliance upon state government in matters of student and institutional rights, restricting the federal domain to those areas—such as collection of defaulted student loans—which touch directly upon the federal commerce and spending powers and which are out of the purview of the states
- Make procedural compliance with existing laws and regulations easier for institutions and students by reducing, where possible, needless diversity in policies

- Halt further "consumer" legislation until such time as the flood of new and existing regulations can be evaluated
- Eliminate procedural regulations which substantively infringe upon academic programming
- Be more aggressive in collecting loan repayments and in bringing delinquent cases to court
- Remove the onus of anti-loan abuse legislation from institutions and place it squarely on the shoulders of defaulting students, except as institutions encourage such abuse
- Pass laws, where they have not yet been adopted, allowing the Internal Revenue Service to turn over to the Department of Health, Education, and Welfare and the Veterans Administration the current addresses of loan defaulters
- Fully fund broad-based Educational Information Centers, created by the Education Amendments of 1976 and currently being initiated on a small scale, to provide a complete range of educational information, guidance, and referral services to all people and schools desiring to use these services in every state
- Subject accrediting association petitions for Office of Education recognition to stricter scrutiny by establishing minimum submission requirements, visiting a greater proportion of member institutions, examining visiting team reports more thoroughly, actively soliciting outside opinions on associations and their member schools, and appointing to the Division of Eligibility and Agency Evaluation Advisory Committee the best qualified people in the country

Appendix A

Key Resources and How to Get Them

1. Education Commission of the State's Model State Legislation for approval of postsecondary educational institutions and authorization to grant degrees.

   Write: Education Commission of the States
   300 Lincoln Tower
   1860 Lincoln Street
   Denver, Colorado 80203

   Call: (303 893-5200

2. Examples of Better Information college catalogs:
   For the Barat College Prospectus

   Write: Theodore Marchese, Director
   Institutional Research, Barat College
   Lake Forest, Illinois 60045

   For the University of California, Irvine, Prospectus

   Write: Office of University and Student Affairs
   University of California, Irvine
   Irvine, California 92664

   For a discussion of how to develop such catalogs and the experiences of 11 demonstration institutions, request *Better Information for Student Choice: Report of a National Task Force.*

   Write: American Association for Higher Education
   One Dupont Circle, Suite 780
   Washington, D.C. 20036

3. Examples of institutional codes of rights and responsibilities:
For a model statement on Fair Practice for Institutions of
Higher Education
Read: "Toward a Statement of Fair Practice" by Elaine H.
El-Khawas in *AGB Reports,* September-October
1978, or
Write: Elaine El-Khawas, Office on Self-Regulation
Initiatives
One Dupont Circle
Washington, D.C. 20036
For the "University of Pittsburgh Guidelines on Academic
Integrity: Student and Faculty Obligations and Hearing Pro-
cedures"
Write: Office of the Chancellor
University of Pittsburgh
Pittsburgh, Pennsylvania 15260
For "A Code of Fair Practice for the University of Monte-
vallo"
Write: Office of the President
University of Montevallo
Montevallo, Alabama 35115
4. Institutional Codes on Admissions:
For "Statement of Principles of Good Practice"
Write: National Association of College Admission Counselors
9933 Lawler, Suite 500
Skokie, Illinois 60076
For "Principles of Board Practice With Reference to College
Admissions"
Write: College Entrance Examination Board
888 Seventh Avenue
New York, New York 10019
5. For a self-administered study form to evaluate college and
university irresponsibility, "Institutional Self-Study Form
for Postsecondary Institutions"
Write: Postsecondary Program Division
Office of Evaluation on Dissemination
U.S. Office of Education
Washington, D.C. 20202

6. Student Consumer information about what to look for in choosing a college:

   For "Look Out for Yourself!: Helpful Hints for Selecting a School or College"

   Write: Office of the Assistant Secretary for Education
   U.S. Department of Health, Education, and Welfare
   Washington, D.C. 20202

   For *Safe Guarding Your Education: A Consumer Guide to College and Occupational Education* by J. Hamilton, J. Wolff, S. Jung, and C. Dayton

   Write: Time Share/Houghton Mifflin
   Hanover, New Hampshire 03755

7. Guidelines on awarding educational credits and credentials:

   For "Recommendations on Credentialing Educational Accomplishments"

   Write: Sales Office
   American Council on Education
   One Dupont Circle
   Washington, D.C. 20036

Appendix B

Carnegie Council Studies Used in This Report

The Carnegie Commission and the Carnegie Council have undertaken several studies related to this report. They are referred to in this volume as Carnegie Surveys, 1969-70; Carnegie Surveys, 1975-76; Catalog Study, 1976; and Carnegie Surveys, 1978.

The "Carnegie Surveys, 1969-70" were conducted under the auspices of the Carnegie Commission on Higher Education with the cooperation of the American Council on Education and support from the U.S. Office of Education. They probed the opinions and experiences of 60,000 faculty, 70,000 undergraduates, and 30,000 graduate students. The technical details of the survey and the survey questionnaires can be found in Martin Trow (Ed.), *Teachers and Students: Aspects of American Higher Education* (New York: McGraw-Hill, 1976).

The "Carnegie Surveys, 1975-76" were conducted by the Carnegie Council on Policy Studies in Higher Education and involved 25,000 faculty members, 25,000 undergraduates, and 25,000 graduate students. The questions used in these surveys and the survey details are discussed in a *Technical Report: 1975 Carnegie Council National Surveys of Higher Education,* by Judy Roizen, Oliver Fulton, and Martin Trow (Berkeley, Calif.: Center for Studies in Higher Education, University of California, 1978).

The "Catalog Study, 1976" was a staff analysis of 1975 catalogs from a representative sample of 270 two- and four-year colleges and universities.

The "Carnegie Surveys, 1978" were conducted under the auspices of the Carnegie Council and involved a comprehensive study of how a representative sample of 586 two- and four-year colleges and universities were adapting to the 1970s. The survey instruments and the details of the survey will be discussed in a forthcoming technical report.

References

Andrews, G. *Assessing Nontraditional Education.* Vol. 1. Washington, D.C.: Council on Postsecondary Accreditation, 1978.

Arnstein, G. "Two Cheers for Accreditation." *Phi Delta Kappan,* January 1979, *60* (5), 357-361.

Assistant Secretary for Education. *Look Out for Yourself: Helpful Hints on Selecting a School or College.* Washington, D.C.: U.S. Government Printing Office, 1977.

Atelsek, F. J., and Gomberg, I. L. *Estimated Number of Student Aid Recipients 1976-1977.* Higher Education Panel Report No. 36. Washington, D.C.: American Council on Education, 1977.

Bailey, S. K. *College Programs on Military Bases,* forthcoming.

Bear, J. *College Degrees by Mail: A Comprehensive Guide to Nontraditional Degree Programs.* Mendicino, Calif.: Rafton and Bear, 1978.

Boffey, P. M. "5 of Boston's 'Big 8' Universities Took No Action Against Students Involved in Term-Paper Scandal." *Chronicle of Higher Education,* March 25, 1974, p. 1.

Boldt, R. F. *Trends in Aptitudes of Graduate Students in Science.* Washington, D.C.: National Science Foundation, 1977.

Bow, J. "Davis, the Only UC Campus with Honor System, Prepares to Revise Its Code." *Sacramento Bee,* August 3, 1975, p. D-5.

"California Law Bars Diploma-Sales Companies." *Chronicle of Higher Education,* October 10, 1978, p. 2.

Carnegie Foundation for the Advancement of Teaching, The. *Missions of the College Curriculum: A Contemporary Review with Suggestions.* San Francisco: Jossey-Bass, 1977.

Carnegie Surveys, 1969-70. This project is discussed in Appendix B.

Carnegie Surveys, 1975-76. This project is discussed in Appendix B.

Carnegie Surveys, 1978. This project is discussed in Appendix B.

Catalog Study, 1976. This research is discussed in Appendix B.

"Charges of Admissions Peddling Prompt Federal and State Probes." *Chronicle of Higher Education,* May 22, 1978, p. 3.

College Entrance Examination Board. *Making It Count: A Report on a Project to Provide Better Financial Aid Information to Students.* Princeton, N.J.: College Entrance Examination Board, 1977.

"Colleges Warned of Danger in Admitting Foreign Students Who Lack Qualifications." *Chronicle of Higher Education,* Sept. 11, 1977, p. 6.

"Court Says No Transcripts for Bankrupt Student Debtors." *Higher Education Daily,* September 20, 1977, p. 5.

"Crack Down on Cheaters, New York Colleges Told." *Chronicle of Higher Education,* March 25, 1974, p. 8.

Daily Californian, August 4, 1978, p. 17.

Dayton, C. W., and Jung, S. M. "Field Test of the Institutional Self-Study Form." Palo Alto, Calif.: American Institutes for Research, 1978.

"Degree-Mill Operator Charged in Illinois." *Chronicle of Higher Education,* July 10, 1978, p. 2.

"Education Centers in New York Called Academically Deficient." *Higher Education Daily,* April 3, 1978, p. 1.

Education Commission of the States. *Consumer Protection in Postsecondary Education: Conference Report and Recommendations.* No. 53. Denver, Colo., 1974.

Education Commission of the States. *Consumer Protection in Postsecondary Education: Report of the National Conference.* No. 64. Denver, Colo., 1975.

El-Khawas, E. "Solving Problems Through Self-Regulation." *Educational Record,* Fall 1978, *59* (4), 323-331.

El-Khawas, E. "Toward a Statement of Fair Practice." *AGB Reports,* September-October 1978, pp. 37-40.

"Ethics Courses Added to West Point Curriculum." *Chronicle of Higher Education,* September 5, 1978, p. 21.

"Extension of GSL Policy Proposed in New Regulations." *Higher Education Daily,* July 20, 1978, pp. 3-4.

"Extensive Critique of Extensions." *New York Times,* April 2, 1976, Section 4, p. 6.

Federal Interagency Committee on Education Subcommittee on Consumer Protection. *Toward a Federal Strategy for Protection of the Consumer of Education.* Washington, D.C.: U.S. Department of Health, Education, and Welfare, 1975.

Federal Interagency Committee on Education. *Keeping Your School or College Catalog in Compliance with Federal Laws and Regulations.* Washington, D.C.: U.S. Government Printing Office, 1978.

"Figure in Scandal Sentenced to Prison." *Chronicle of Higher Education,* August 7, 1978, p. 2.

Finkin, M. *Federal Reliance on Educational Accreditation: The Scope of Administrative Discretion.* Washington, D.C.: Council on Postsecondary Accreditation, 1978.

"For $45, You Can Buy a Fake Stanford Degree." *Chronicle of Higher Education,* May 8, 1978, p. 14.

"Former Financial Aid Officer Charged with Embezzlement." *Chronicle of Higher Education,* September 26, 1977, p. 2.

Fund for the Improvement of Postsecondary Education. *Resources for Change: A Guide to Projects 1976-77.* Washington, D.C.: U.S. Government Printing Office, 1976.

Hamilton, J. A., Wolff, J. M., Jung, S. M., and Dayton, C. W. *Safeguarding Your Education.* Santa Ana, Calif.: Media One, 1977.

Hendrick, C., and Murfin, M. E. "Project Library Ripoff: Study of Periodical Mutilation in University Library." *College and Research Libraries,* November 1974, *35,* 402-411.

"HEW to Extend Checks for GSL Defaulters to Military Personnel." *Higher Education Daily,* October 13, 1978, p. 4.

"HEW Tightens Control Over Student Aid Programs." *Memo,* March 17, 1978, p. 2.

"HEW to Step Up Collection of Direct Loans." *Higher Education Daily,* November 15, 1978, p. 3.

"Iowa Regents Will Allow Universities to Advertise." *Chronicle of Higher Education,* January 17, 1977, p. 2.

"Johns Hopkins Scraps Honor Code." *Los Angeles Times,* July 28, 1975, Section I, p. 2.

Jung, S. M., Hamilton, J. A., Helliwell, C. B., Gross, D. E., Bloom, N. L., Shearer, J. W., and McBain, S. L. *Improving the Consumer Protection Function in Postsecondary Education.* Palo Alto, Calif.: American Institutes for Research, 1976.

Jung, S. M., Hamilton, J., Helliwell, C. B., and Wheeler, J. D. *A Study of State Oversight in Postsecondary Education.* Palo Alto, Calif.: American Institutes for Research, 1977.

Jung, S. M., Hamilton, J. A., Helliwell, C. B., and Wheeler, J. D. *Executive Summary of Final Report: A Study of State Oversight in Postsecondary Education.* Palo Alto, Calif.: American Institutes for Research, 1977a.

Kaplin, W. A. *The Law of Higher Education: Legal Implications of Administrative Decision Making.* San Francisco: Jossey-Bass, 1978.

Kintzer, F. C. *Middleman in Higher Education: Improving Articulation Among High School, Community College, and Senior Institutions.* San Francisco: Jossey-Bass, 1973.

Levine, A. *Handbook on Undergraduate Curriculum.* San Francisco: Jossey-Bass, 1978.

Levine, A., and Weingart, J. *Reform of Undergraduate Education.* San Francisco: Jossey-Bass, 1973.

"Light-Fingered Library Patrons Cost U.S. Taxpayers." *Library Scene,* June 1976, pp. 28-29.

London, H. *The Culture of a Community College.* New York: Praeger, 1978.

Magarrell, J. "Are Colleges Training Computer Criminals?" *Chronicle of Higher Education,* July 17, 1978, p. 1.

Manning, W. H. "Is the Ability of College Seniors Declining?" Report to the American Assembly of Collegiate Schools of Business, April 30, 1976.

Marchese, T. M. "Questions and Answers About Barat's Prospectus." Barat College, Lake Forrest, Ill., 1976 (Mimeograph).

Marchese, T. M. "Better Information About Student Choice: The Basic Argument." Keynote address at the National Conference on Better Information for Student Choice, Washington, D.C., March 30, 1977.

"Maryland Term-Paper Ban Ruled Unconstitutional." *Chronicle of Higher Education,* August 18, 1975, p. 2.

Middleton, L. "Union for Experimenting Colleges Face Crisis, Receivership Sought." *Chronicle of Higher Education,* July 17, 1978, p. 1.

Muñoz, D. G., and Garcia-Bahne, B. "A Study of the Chicano Experience in Higher Education." An unpublished report for the Center for Minority Group Mental Health Programs, National Institute of Mental Health, Bethesda, Md., 1978.

National Advisory Council on Education Professions Development. *Gatekeepers in Education: A Report on Institutional Licensing.* Washington, D.C., April 1975.

"National Crime Wave Plagues University Libraries." *Chronicle of Higher Education,* August 9, 1976, p. 5.

National Student Educational Fund. *The Options Handbook.* 3 vols. Washington, D.C., 1976.

National Task Force on Better Information for Student Choice. *Better Information for Student Choice: Report of a National Task Force.* Washington, D.C.: American Association for Higher Education, 1978.

"New York Tightens 'Emancipated Student' Definition." *Higher Education Daily,* July 8, 1976, p. 3.

"OE Planning Changes in BEOG Validation Procedures for Colleges." *Higher Education Daily,* June 23, 1978, p. 5.

"OE Proposes to Clean Up Student Aid Programs." *Higher Education Daily,* August 16, 1978, p. 5.

"OE Proposes New BEOG Regulations to Clarify Procedures, Clamp Down on Cheaters." *Higher Education Daily,* May 16, 1978, p. 4.

"OE Rejecting Three Times as Many BEOG Applications This Year." *Higher Education Daily,* August 22, 1978, p. 1.

Orlans, H., Levin, N. J., Bauer, E. K., and Arnstein, G. E. *Private Accreditation and Public Eligibility.* Washington, D.C.: Brookings Institution, 1974.

"PA Arrests Students on Loan-Fraud Charges." *Chronicle of Higher Education,* August 9, 1976, p. 2.

Peterson, I. "Race for Grades Revives Among College Students; Cheating and Anxiety Rise." *New York Times,* November 21, 1974, p. 1.

Peterson, R. G. "The Catalog as a Contract." *Educational Record,* Summer 1970, pp. 260-266.

"Queens College Uncovers Grade Tampering Scheme." *Chronicle of Higher Education,* March 13, 1978, p. 2.

Roark, A. C. "GAO Urges Quick Action on Loans to Beat Statute of Limitations." *Chronicle of Higher Education,* September 6, 1977, p. 14.

"Rules Proposed for Participation in Aid Programs." *Higher Education and National Affairs,* August 11, 1978, p. 5.

"Senate Panel Clears Ban on Student Loan Bankruptcies." *Higher Education Daily,* July 25, 1978, p. 3.

"Some Colleges Are Bobbing Up Everywhere." *New York Times,* January 7, 1979, p. 20.

Southern Regional Education Board. *State Regulation of Off-Campus Programs and Out-of-State Institutions.* No. 12. Atlanta, 1978.

Special Subcommittee on Education (House of Representatives). *Federal Higher Education Programs Institutional Eligibility.* Washington, D.C.: U.S. Government Printing Office, 1974.

Stark, J. S. "Is More Information Better?" In J. S. Stark (Ed.), *New Direc-*

tions for Higher Education: Promoting Consumer Protection for Students, no. 13. San Francisco: Jossey-Bass, 1976.

Stark, J. S. (Ed.). *New Directions for Higher Education: Promoting Consumer Protection for Students*, no. 13. San Francisco: Jossey-Bass, 1976a.

Stark, J. S. *The Many Faces of Educational Consumerism*. Lexington, Mass.: Heath, 1977.

Stark, J. S., and Marchese, T. M. "Auditing College Publications for Perspective Students." *Journal of Higher Education*, January-February 1978, *49* (1), 82-92.

"State Agencies Tracking Down Employees with Defaulted Loans." *Higher Education Daily*, September 1, 1978, p. 5.

Stecher, C. "CLEP and the Great Credit Giveaway." *Change*, 1977, *9* (3), 36-41.

Steif, W. "Education Officials to Tackle Lowering of Degree's Worth." *Rocky Mountain News*, July 10, 1978, p. 9.

"Student Bankruptcies Rejected by New York Judges." *Chronicle of Higher Education*, May 9, 1977, p. 6.

"Term Paper Companies Claim Persecution by Academia, Seek Respectability." *Higher Education Daily*, February 4, 1977, p. 2.

"Texas Student-Aid Officer Indicated on Fraud Charge." *Chronicle of Higher Education*, November 28, 1977, p. 2.

"203,068 Foreign Students Enroll at U.S. Colleges: 23,310 from Iran." *Chronicle of Higher Education*, April 17, 1978, p. 13.

"Two-Year Colleges Lead in NDSL Defaults." *Higher Education Daily*, March 28, 1978, p. 1.

U.S. House of Representatives, Subcommittee on Postsecondary Education. *Oversight Hearings on All Forms of Federal Student Financial Assistance*. Washington, D.C.: U.S. Government Printing Office, 1977.

U.S. National Center for Education Statistics. *The Condition of Education: 1978 Edition*. Washington, D.C.: U.S. Government Printing Office, 1978.

U.S. Office of Education. "National Direct Student Loan Program: Status of Defaults as of June 30, 1977." Washington, D.C., February 9, 1978.

U.S. Senate. *Report of the Committee on Veterans Affairs, United States Senate to Accompany S.969*. Washington, D.C.: U.S. Government Printing Office, 1976.

"Unsuccessful Medical School Applicant Wins Fraud Suit Against College." *Higher Education Daily*, January 16, 1978, p. 4.

"Vanderbilt Ordered to Pay Former Doctoral Students." *Chronicle of Higher Education*, September 6, 1977.

Van Dyne, L. "Principal Figure in Scandal Is Still Waiting for His Trial: Institute and 2 Colleges Were Financially Ruined." *Chronicle of Higher Education*, August 7, 1978, p. 2.

"VA Proposes Rules for Processing School Liability Cases." *Higher Education Daily*, January 20, 1978, pp. 3-4.

"VA Education Loans Hit 44 Percent Default Rate, GAO Reports." *Higher Education Daily*, May 17, 1978, p. 1.

Watkins, B. "Educational Brokers: Threat to Academic Standards?" *Chronicle of Higher Education*, June 20, 1977, p. 6.

"Whatever Happened to the 'C'?" *Brown Alumni Monthly*, May-June 1973, pp. 14-15.

Willett, S. L. "Information on Federal Student Assistance: Its Availability, Price, and Other Unfinished Business." Unpublished report for the Office of Consumer Affairs, Department of Health, Education, and Welfare, Washington, D.C., March 1976.

Winkler, K. "Eighteen Doctoral Programs Ordered Ended by Louisiana Regents." *Chronicle of Higher Education*, November 8, 1976, p. 9.

Winkler, K. "State's Power to Close Ph.D. Program Is Upheld by a New York Court." *Chronicle of Higher Education*, January 31, 1977, p. 1.

Index